Mark W

The Pocket Essential

ROGER CORMAN

www.pocketessentials.com

First published in Great Britain 2003 by
Pocket Essentials, P O Box 394, Harpenden, Herts, AL5 1XJ, UK

Distributed in the USA by Trafalgar Square Publishing,
PO Box 257, Howe Hill Road, North Pomfret, Vermont 05053

Copyright © Mark Whitehead 2003
Series Editor: David Mathew

A CIP catalogue record for this book is available from the British Library.

ISBN 1-904048-10-2

2 4 6 8 10 9 7 5 3 1

Book typeset by Wordsmith Solutions Ltd
Printed and bound by Cox & Wyman

For mum and dad, who let me stay up late enough to see many of these films in the first place, and for Miriam, who helped above and beyond.

Acknowledgements

My thanks to Karen Tanner, Dave Holifield, Richard Hague and Craig Edwards (where are you?) for finding films I'd given up on. Tips of the hat are also due to Ian Brown, Shannon Perry, Ion Mills, Paul Duncan and Steve Holland. This book wouldn't be what it is without you. Make of that what you will.

CONTENTS

Introduction: Roger Who?

'(Corman is) A man who feels saying "Thank you very much" after each set-up is optional because it wastes two seconds.'

Jonathan Demme

Since its proper arrival in the Fifties, television had taken on Hollywood and won. The Sixties saw cinema audience figures at an all-time low. Although the figures would rise towards the end of the decade, in 1969 audiences were at only 25% of the figure for 1946. There were also fewer movies being made. In 1959 there were 187 movies released, barely half the amount released in 1950. At this point nearly 75% of Hollywood employees were engaged in work for television rather than cinema. While the Hollywood majors saw the Sixties as a time of crisis, one independent studio triumphed. American International Pictures (AIP) survived and flourished by aiming its movies at the key cinema-going demographic: teenagers and young adults. Since its birth in 1954, AIP had been run by James H Nicholson and Samuel Z Arkoff. Their formula for success was simple: cheaply-made movies released as double bills for drive-in and independent cinemas that were excluded from showing the output of the Hollywood majors. For AIP, no subject went unexploited, no bandwagon was left un-jumped and the more topical the subject was, the better. From the anodyne 'beach party' movies (e.g. *Beach Party*, *Beach Blanket Bingo*, etc) to the later Vietnam-influenced youth rebellion movies such as *The Trip* and *Wild In The Streets*, Arkoff and Nicholson gave their audiences exactly what they wanted to see and ensured that they would come back for more. AIP's greatest asset in achieving this goal was their most prolific director during the Fifties and Sixties: Roger Corman.

Roger who? This is a phrase that I have encountered with depressing regularity while writing this book. 'You know…' I probe weakly, 'the guy who directed those Edgar Allan Poe/Vincent Price movies in the Sixties…' And suddenly everyone lights up. 'Oh yeah… I loved those when I was a kid.' Of course you did. The name never really stuck because Corman was never really a candidate for auteur theory. Too many people did too many things on his films for him to be an auteur. But once you realise that, then you start to realise that Hitch was at his best with Saul Bass and Bernard Herrmann, that Scorsese needed Michael Chapman and De Niro, that Godard needed Coutard, that the auteur theory is fatally flawed… Corman had Floyd Crosby (cinematography), Daniel Haller (art direction), Ronalds Stein and

Sinclair (music, editing), Marjorie Corso (costumes) – all of them weaving magic out of a budget that would make the likes of James Cameron or Ron Howard break down and weep like babies. And speaking of whom, guess where those two got their first break. Corman. Along with Coppola, Scorsese, Demme, Nicholson... A generation of Hollywood's great and good launched courtesy of a man that most people these days can barely recall.

Corman is often called 'The King of The Bs' (or less flatteringly 'King Of The Zs'), a term that, he points out, is inaccurate. The 'B' movie was a product of the Depression. Created to lure audiences back to the cinemas, they were made cheaply, with untested (or fading) talent and formed a double bill with an 'A'-list movie. By the time Corman started directing, the 'B' had been killed off by TV and adult cinema-goers' preferences for the bigger-budget movies. Interestingly, Corman's first movies were Westerns, something that had been bread and butter to Republic Pictures, one of the great B-movie studios.

My first memory of Roger Corman is probably very similar to many people of my age group. No, I'm not telling. Just getting into horror movies, I would wait every year for BBC2 to run their summer horror double bills. What I could rent on video was mainly all sheep guts and dubbed actors (Argento, Fulci, Lenzi, Deodato); what BBC2 gave me was the subtle stuff. One year, Universal from the Thirties, then the suggestive noir-horrors of Val Lewton, and then the Technicolor terror of Corman's Poe adaptations. Each season was a revelation, but Corman's *The Masque Of The Red Death* blew me away. Having recently seen *Don't Look Now* and *The Wicker Man*, here was a movie that combined the colour coding of one with the theological complexity of the other and preceded both of them. Yeah, and it had Vincent Price (I'd seen *Theatre Of Blood* quite recently as well – at the Windsor ABC quintuple-bill all-nighter, now a TSB). It's all nostalgia and if I'm not connecting then I apologise, but this season in my mind made Corman's name synonymous with Lewton, Whale, Fisher and Argento.

Corman, of course, tends to be undervalued because he worked quickly, cheaply and frequently within the confines of genre cinema – an area from which, many mainstream critics still insist, little of great value is produced. So I'll go for broke. Roger Corman made as many films as Alfred Hitchcock, but in 15 years rather than 50. While I'm making no great claims that Corman was better, or even as good as Hitch, they both had their share of clinkers and they both produced enduring works of cinema particularly in their middle period. Both were shrewd observers of cinematic trends and both, at the height of their powers, produced complex and *coherent* films that continue to fascinate and have never, despite continuing attempts and attacks, been bettered. Watch *Vertigo* back to back with *The Tomb Of Ligeia* and tell me it ain't so.

But before Hitchcock fans come to lynch me, Corman never really publicized himself. He didn't have a vision that he wanted to be recorded for posterity. He was a particularly American product and more particularly a product of AIP. If you could buck the trend, great. If you could start a trend, even better. But at the end of the day, if you could make a profit on something that cost next to nothing to make, excellent. He never allowed himself more time or money than was needed and perhaps that is the greatest shame about Corman. While he was rising to the challenges of a two-day shoot (*The Little Shop Of Horrors*) or making a third film on a budget allotted for two (*The Creature From The Haunted Sea*), he rarely gave himself space to see what he really could achieve on a sensible timescale with a sensible budget. Watching *Frankenstein Unbound*, his first, and last, directing job in nearly twenty years, you get the feeling that he's just crying out for someone to tell him: 'Hey, Roger, we need to get this in the cinemas by next weekend'.

Whenever you read in the gossip columns of a movie star's latest hissy-fit over the size of the Winnebago or the temperature of the mineral water, it is satisfying to think about how things might have been if they had been working for Corman during his boom period. Anything more guaranteed to smack the raging ego out of them has probably not yet been invented and once the time machine to do the job has been built and tested, we would be doing the whole entertainment universe a favour by packing the prima donnas into it and sending them back. Allison Hayes only got out of *Oklahoma Woman* by breaking her arm, Dick Miller was smacked senseless by a demented (and not very good) method actor on *Carnival Rock;* everyone, from Corman down, was expected to perform as many jobs as necessary in order to get the film made, whether acting, set-striking or performing unofficial stunt work. If you had an attitude, you could leave it at the studio door. Those in for the long haul soon adjusted, those who didn't were not invited back.

Given the economic and time constraints that Corman found or placed himself under (one example among many: *The Terror* in which principle photography was completed over three days because Boris Karloff owed him three days work after *The Raven* had wrapped early), it's a wonder that he turned out so many films that are still enjoyable. His contemporaries are the names from a thousand cult movie magazines: Herschell Gordon Lewis, Ray Dennis Steckler, Al Adamson, Ted V Mikels… But the problem with a lot of cult movies, especially of this type, is that once the initial amusement has worn off, they get a bit… well, dull. While, sadly, most of Corman's films do not achieve cinematic greatness, there are few of his films that are dull. Even something as muddled as *The Terror* still manages to entertain.

Anyone flicking through this book in advance will discover that much of it is anecdotal, rather than analytical. With Corman's movies this is unavoidable. Producing films at a rate that would make even the likes of William 'one-shot' Beaudine blanch, Corman jumped from genre to genre, wherever the audience's tastes led him and AIP. However, there are themes that emerge. One is that of vision, particularly distortions of eyesight, and he returns to it from *Not Of This Earth* onwards. But Corman's main theme can be discerned in his continual fascination with society's outsiders. It first emerged in his second movie as producer, *The Fast And The Furious*, where the characters played by John Ireland (an escaped convict) and Dorothy Malone (barred from entering motor races because she is a woman) are presented sympathetically. Corman is silent as to what this theme means to him, but AIP's target audience may well hold the key. Teenagers in the Fifties represented a growing consumer culture that had been created by the post-war boom. The 'teenager' was a borderline category, neither child nor adult. With this group, 'discovered' film-makers (and artists in other media) began to feature characters with whom teens could identify. The Fifties were the years of the rise of market research and Madison Avenue, after all. The archetypal teenager was a rebel, an outsider, no longer a child yet excluded from adult recreations, such as sex and alcohol, by the authority figures of the state and the family. Alienated by the clean-cut teen representations of Sally Field's *Gidget* and Disney's Mouseketeers, teens turned towards exploitation cinema for role models. Corman's movies frequently carried objective portrayals of the borderline characters in society. With his films that are targeted at drive-in cinemas, a main haunt of teenagers, one can see how his portrayals of outsiders' experiences (of isolation and transgression) were eagerly received by a teenage audience. This aided his commercial success. A similar feat was pulled off by pseudonymous pulp novelist Richard Allen and his 'Skinhead' series in the early Seventies.

Despite thematic continuities, Corman was rarely involved in the screenwriting process beyond occasionally suggesting story ideas. His writers knew how to get the best out of an idea – whether it was mutant sea life, hopped-up teens or Gothic excess. Charles B Griffith was the most prolific of the collaborators. Occasionally working with Mark Hanna, Griffith produced the scripts for Corman's cultier successes, most famously *A Bucket Of Blood* and *The Little Shop Of Horrors*. Other names appear less frequently but know the terrain: R Wright Campbell, Richard Matheson, author of *I Am Legend*, *The (Incredible) Shrinking Man* and *Nightmare At 30,000 Feet*. (You know, that episode of *The Twilight Zone* where William

Shatner sees a gremlin tearing at the fuselage of the plane he's riding on. You loved it as a kid.) Ray Russell, author of *Mr Sardonicus* and *Incubus*. And Charles Beaumont. An incredibly gifted writer, Beaumont died at 38 of Alzheimer's disease. In 1989, Corman's New Concorde company financed the filming of his unfinished screenplay, *Paranoid*. Directed by Adam Simon as *Brain Dead*, it starred Bills Pullman and Paxton, and Bud Cort. This underrated movie is arguably the only other horror film to follow *Videodrome*'s train of thought to its bitter conclusion and stands as an impressive tribute to Beaumont's talent. Other writers for Corman include George Armitage, director of *Grosse Point Blank* and Robert Towne, who would write *Chinatown*, which stars Jack Nicholson, who also wrote the script for Corman's *The Trip*. When people tire of Kevin Bacon, they can always try Six Degrees Of Roger Corman.

For instance, it was New World that introduced the Cronenberg virus into the USA by distributing *Shivers* when Canada was still having conniption fits over their child's product. Corman is also inextricably linked with the history of *The Wicker Man*. Corman was sent a 16mm print by Michael Deeley, then head of its UK distributors, British Lion. Corman offered him $50,000 for the distribution rights but told him the picture was a little slow. Deeley, who hated the film, asked how he could improve it and Corman offered several off-the-cuff cuts he thought would speed up the movie. Deeley followed Corman's suggestions, hacking the movie from 102 minutes down to an 84-minute second feature, released with *Don't Look Now*. Corman lost out on the distribution deal but, later, he inadvertently helped in the picture's restoration when the same print Deeley had sent him was discovered still in New World's vaults.

And this unique example pins down precisely the dilemma with Corman. Is he a great artist or just a shrewd businessman? Has he continued to prove himself by backing new talent or has he just surrounded himself with talented college graduates with impressive degrees, merely to impose his own theories and bask in their glory? There is no doubt that his directorial career includes truly great films, such as *The Fall Of The House Of Usher* and *The Masque Of The Red Death;* several of his films, such as *A Bucket of Blood* and *The Little Shop Of Horrors*, came about from self-enforced austerity and resulted in thoroughly enjoyable, truly quirky movies. Others, such as *Atlas* and *She-Gods Of Shark Reef*, are dogs. This also applies to his bigger-budget movies: *The St Valentine's Day Massacre* remains one of the great gangster pictures, *The Secret Invasion* is appalling. Many New World films are very enjoyable, New Concorde-Horizon material less so. You get the feeling that you are watching an inveterate gambler nearing the end of his lucky streak.

Corman's New World Pictures was for the Seventies what New Line was for the Eighties and Miramax for the Nineties – ballsy independent companies chugging out fast entertainment product with an eye on the current trends. Both of them followed Corman in distributing 'difficult' foreign movies to American audiences and garnering kudos. Corman even cameoed in Miramax's *Scream 3* (via sub-company Dimension, founded by Corman alumni Stephanie Rothman) as a studio executive, frustrated at the stalled production of his cash-in on the Woodsboro murders. Joe Dante gave him an equally sour cameo in *The Howling* (see chapter 7).

What you come away with when researching Corman is a picture of a man capable of great things who, becoming inured to working under stifling financial and time constrictions, never allowed himself the luxury of breathing; a man obsessed with attaching himself to those who promised greatness but who, allowing himself a little slack, would have been capable of it himself. For Hollywood, he tuned up some of the greatest directors that they had ever seen, but they never accepted him as one of their own. It's no surprise that the favoured theme of his movies is society's outsider.

1: Early Days

'A...director friend of mine once related how he visited a Paramount set where Billy Wilder was shooting a big-budget film with Jack Lemmon. He wandered over to watch one of the masters at work. At lunch, back on his own set, someone asked what he had seen them doing. And he said, 'They spent the morning lighting a close-up on Lemmon.'

Roger Corman,
How I Made A Hundred Movies In Hollywood
And Never Lost A Dime.

Roger William Corman was born in Detroit on April 5th 1926. Later, the family moved to Beverley Hills. Roger and brother Gene both took an interest in drama and performed in school plays at Beverley Hills High. These interests were set aside when he graduated in 1943 and went to study engineering at Stanford, his ambition being to follow in his father's footsteps. During his time at Stanford, he became a freelance writer publishing articles in *Popular Mechanics* and *Science and Mechanics* before enrolling for officer training in the US Navy. After World War II, he returned to Stanford under the GI Bill, graduating in 1947 with an industrial engineering degree.

Returning to LA, Roger realised that he was more interested in films than engineering and, after three days work at US Electrical Motors, he quit and began the slog to break into the movie industry. In 1948, he got a job as a messenger boy at Twentieth Century-Fox and was promoted to story analyst after six months. Hearing that the studio was looking for an offbeat Western for Gregory Peck, Corman recalled seeing a script called 'The Big Gun'. He annotated it with his own corrections and handed it to an executive. The suggestion worked, and Peck starred in *The Gunfighter* in 1950 (director Henry King). Corman received no benefits for passing on the script. He decided to return to university. This time he spent a term at Oxford under the GI Bill and then bummed around Europe for a year, where he learned something about wheeling and dealing by smuggling cameras across the Swiss border and selling them in Paris at a profit.

Returning to the US, his story editor at Fox gave him a good reference for a job at the Jules Goldin agency. After a short time there, and then as a grip at a local TV station, Corman moved to the Dick Highland Agency. It was here that he got his first major break. He sold a script entitled 'The House Under The Sea' to Allied Artists for $3,500. Retitled *Highway Drag-*

net to cash in on the success of the TV series, it starred Richard Conte and Joan Bennett and was directed by Nathan Juran. Corman worked for nothing on the set, earning himself credits both as writer and associate producer. However, the film treated his central idea (a shoot-out in a flooded house) so badly that he thought the film was going to bomb and his movie career was dead. But *Highway Dragnet* did reasonably well at the box office. It also showed Corman that few films are ever complete successes or utter turkeys. Taking this as a positive sign, he rented a 'production office' (actually a reception for a proper office over the Cock 'n' Bull Restaurant on Sunset Boulevard) for $25 a month and began to work on his first production.

Corman started in 1954 with *The Monster From The Ocean Floor*. Budgeted at $12,000, he financed it with $3,500 earned from *Highway Dragnet*, along with shares that he sold to friends. Corman was still $2,000 short when he met Wyott Ordung, an acting student who wanted to break into directing. Corman let him direct *Monster* in return for $2,000 which Ordung had earned scripting the cult *Robot Monster*. Corman's movie was further helped by Sid Solo, the president of Consolidated Laboratories, who agreed to defer the $5,000 developing and printing costs until the film was released. *Monster*'s major coup (and partly its inspiration) was the use of a mini-submarine that is used to kill the *Monster*. Corman contacted the sub's makers, Aerojet General, after reading about it in the *LA Times*, and struck a deal whereby he would get free use of the sub for his movie in return for product placement and a credit for the company.

For the shoot, Corman acted as producer, grip and driver, setting the pattern for many of his films. The cast was bolstered with the first screen appearance of Jonathan Haze. Haze, a fine character actor, would become part of Corman's unofficial rep company. At the time of *Monster*, Haze was working at a Tide gas station on Santa Monica Boulevard where he was spotted by Ordung, a regular customer. Ordung convinced him that there was a role in his movie if he grew a moustache. Haze did so and was fired by Tide, but he got the acting gig. He also became stunt advisor for many of Corman's movies.

The film marked the start of Corman's partnership with cinematographer Floyd Crosby. Previously best known for photographing *High Noon*, Crosby would lens many of Corman's movies and give them a look that often belied their low budgets.

Corman's brother, Gene, set up a distribution deal for *Monster* through the Lippert Releasing Company. Another company, Realart (whose sales manager was James H Nicholson), was also interested in distributing the picture but, unlike Lippert, they weren't prepared to offer an advance against their distribution income. Realising that an advance gave him an immediate opportunity to continue making movies, Corman took the $60,000 that Lippert was offering. It allowed him to pay off *Monster*'s debts and left him enough to go straight into production on his next feature, which he had budgeted at $50,000. *The Fast And The Furious* (also 1954) starred John Ireland and Dorothy Malone. Corman hired John Ireland at a reduced fee on the understanding that he could co-direct the movie (along with editor Edward Sansom). The film was shot in nine days, with Corman acting as one of the stunt drivers for the race sequences. Corman further stretched the budget by getting Jaguar to supply racing cars in exchange for prominent product placement. The race footage was filmed at the Jaguar Open Sports Car race at Monterey, with Corman covering one of the two cameras needed to film the race. This experience made him realise that directing was his true calling.

2: Fast And Furious (1954-58)

'With Roger you always worked. I mean, you could have one eye hanging out and he'd just shoot you from another angle.'

Beverly Garland

Corman received distribution offers for *The Fast And The Furious* from Columbia, Republic and Allied Artists. Instead, he went with American Releasing Corporation, who offered him a three-picture deal. It was to be a historic moment in modern cinema. With James Nicholson as president and entertainment lawyer Samuel Arkoff as vice-president, the company would soon become American International Pictures, and Corman would be their most prolific director for the next fourteen years.

Five Guns West (1954)

Cast: John Lund (Govern Sturgess), Dorothy Malone (Shalee), Touch Connors (Hale Clinton), Bob Campbell (John Candy), Jonathan Haze (William Candy), Paul Birch (Haggard), James Stone (Uncle Mime), Jack Ingram (Stephen Jethro), Larry Thor (Southern Captain).

Crew: Director/Producer/Story Roger Corman, Writer R Wright Campbell, Cinematography Floyd Crosby, Music Buddy Bregman, Editor Ronald Sinclair, Art Director Ben Hayne, 78 minutes.

Story: The American Civil War. Five convicted murderers, Sturgess, the Candy brothers, Clinton and Haggard, are pardoned in return for helping the Confederates recapture traitor Jethro and the gold he's taking to the Union. Travelling through Comanche territory, loyalties shift. Plots are hatched to steal the gold when Jethro is captured, with a frail order maintained by Sturgess, the group's self-appointed leader. Planning to ambush Jethro at a way station, the group are further divided by their attraction to the station's female owner, Shalee. Sturgess saves her from their advances on several occasions while making his own feelings known. They finally ambush Jethro, but he has already deposited the gold in a Californian bank. When Sturgess is revealed to be a Confederate officer, the others lay siege to the station. In the ensuing gunfight, the Candys and Clinton are killed and Haggard flees. Sturgess takes Jethro back. He vows to return for Shalee.

Background: This unpretentious variant on a story that would reach its apotheosis in Robert Aldrich's *The Dirty Dozen* was Corman's first film as director and producer. In order to gain some experience of directing beforehand, Corman had borrowed a 16mm camera and lighting equipment from his key grip, Chuck Hannawalt. With Hannawalt acting as director of photography and another friend knocking out a screenplay, Corman gathered together some actors and shot a short film on the beach. Convinced that the footage wasn't great, he never edited the film. With this brief introduction to directing, he set about getting *Five Guns West* underway. For $200, Corman bought stock footage of hoards of movie Indians galloping across the plain. This footage is used in the scene when the five leads enter Comanche country. 'Seeing' the Indians in the distance, the characters decide to go the other way, thus avoiding encountering the Indians and costly movie extras.

Haze got Campbell, a good friend, the script-writing job and Campbell wrote Haze a scenery-chewing psycho role to return the favour. It was Campbell who noticed that Corman was following the script most of the time and advised him to watch what the actors were doing instead. He would continue to write for Corman throughout his directorial career. Campbell, it should be noted, is credited with being the creator of the term 'La-la Land' for LA, in his mystery novel *In La-la Land We Trust*.

Corman decided the best way to get good crew members was to pick out those who did a good job on one movie and hold onto them; he established a crew that would see him through his entire time at AIP. *Five Guns* also saw the arrival of Ronald Sinclair as editor. Sinclair had begun work as an editor the year before, a job that he would continue with until his death in 1992. Outside of working on Corman and Bert I Gordon movies for AIP, he would later edit Bob (*Porky's*) Clark's Vietnam-vet zombie flick *Dead Of Night* and work on *Die Hard* and *Die Hard 2*.

Verdict: A standard oater, *Five Guns* benefits from decent cinematography and sound performances all round. Although wordy, it moves at a brisk pace and several action scenes retain the tension between the characters, particularly at the climax. 3/5

Despite throwing up on his first day from sheer nerves, Corman realised that directing was the job for him. Arkoff and Nicholson agreed, and despite a few glitches at major studios, Corman wasn't out of work for the next fifteen years.

Apache Woman (1955)

Cast: Lloyd Bridges (Rex Moffet), Joan Taylor (Anne Libeau), Lance Fuller (Armand), Morgan Jones (Macy), Paul Birch (Sheriff), Jonathan Haze (Tom Chandler), Paul Dubov (Ben), Lou Place (Carrom Bentley), Gene Marlowe (White Star), Dick Miller (Tall Tree), Chester Conklin (Mooney), Jean Howell (Mrs Chandler).

Crew: Director/Producer Roger Corman, Writer Lou Rusoff, Cinematography Floyd Crosby, Music Ronald Stein, Editor Ronald Sinclair, 82 minutes.

Story: The signing of the Apache Peace Treaty brings an uneasy truce between Settlers and Indians. However, a series of murderous raids on a small town near an Apache reservation disrupts the peace and the townsfolk threaten retaliation. The government, fearing escalating violence, dispatch agent Rex Moffet to investigate. On arrival he intervenes in a knife fight between short-tempered local Tom Chandler and the attractive mixed-race Anne Libeau, enraging the townsfolk with his pacifist stance. Later, Moffet meets Anne again and explains his peace mission. She is suspicious but begins to fall in love with him. When Anne discovers her brother, Armand, and his gang of white renegades are behind the crimes, she is too late to stop Moffet riding into Armand's ambush. In a cliff-top struggle, an unarmed Moffet bests knife-wielding Armand, who falls to his death. The lovers are reunited and peace returns to the communities.

Background: The second of Corman's three-picture deal with the American Releasing Corporation, *Apache Woman* was filmed in colour during a two-week period in which he also made *Five Guns West*. It cost $80,000 and made a profit for the company.

It was the first film for which Ronald Stein provided the score. Having arrived from St Louis hoping to work in motion pictures, he and his wife were on the verge of penury. He had left a recording of some of his music with Corman earlier in the week and the following Sunday received a call. Corman offered him a chance, four hundred dollars, one and a half percent of the producer's profit and 'a credit as big as Dimitri Tiomkin's'. Stein jumped at the chance. All Corman asked for was 'a modern Indian score'. Stein didn't know what he meant, but what he provided for *Apache Woman* pleased Corman and ARC enough to mean that Stein scored almost every AIP picture for the next two years.

Apache Woman also marked the first screen appearance of Dick Miller. Miller had originally come to LA with the intention of being a writer, but after a year of scratching by on meagre sales, he was ready to return to New York. Then he heard from his old friend, Jonathan Haze, who introduced him to Corman. According to Miller, Corman asked him:

'What do you do?'

'I'm a writer. Need any scripts?'

'No, I've got scripts, I need actors.'

'Fine, I'm an actor.'

So Corman cast him as one of the renegade Indians, and then a week later as a cowboy for the same movie. In fact, Miller formed part of the posse that tracked his Indian character down. The tough-looking Miller appeared in over twenty of Corman's films. From the late Seventies, he was adopted as a mascot by several of Corman's alumni, particularly Joe Dante. His appearances post-Corman include the gun-shop owner in *The Terminator* and *Gremlins* where he played alongside *Little Shop Of Horrors* co-star Jackie Joseph.

Verdict: Although examining racial concerns that Corman would return to more dramatically with *The Intruder*, Corman walked onto *Apache Woman* with Rusoff's script already completed. One of Rusoff's more action-packed stories, Corman got him to add an 'outcast' sub-plot, dealing with the problems facing the 'half-breed' characters, disenfranchised from both white and Apache cultures. 3/5

The Oklahoma Woman (1955)

aka *The Yellow Rose Of Texas*

Cast: Richard Denning (Steve Ward), Peggie Castle (Marie 'Oklahoma' Saunders), Tudor Owen (Ed Grant), Martin Kingsley (Sheriff Bill Peters), Cathy Downs (Susan Grant), Touch Connors (Tom Blake), Jonathan Haze, Richard Miller, Thomas Dillon, Edmund Cobb, Bruno Ve Sota.

Crew: Producer/Director Roger Corman, Writer Lou Rusoff, Music Ronald Stein, Editor Ronald Sinclair, Cinematography Fred West, 71 minutes.

Story: Former gunslinger Steve Ward is released from prison. Vowing to reform, he returns to his late grandmother's ranch in Oklahoma. In the nearby town, he is reunited with his old flame, Marie Saunders. On hearing of her life during his absence, Ward declines to reignite their romance. Now the local saloon-keeper, Marie has obtained power and wealth by employing gunslingers to intimidate the townsfolk. One of the gunslingers, Tom Blake, is Ward's old rival for Marie's affections. Marie discovers that Ward has fallen for Susan Grant, whose father is Marie's main opponent. Angered by Marie's jealousy, Blake plots revenge. That night he murders Susan's father, making it look like Ward did the deed. Blake's plan works and the townsfolk organise a necktie party for Ward. However, he is saved at the last minute by Susan, who beats a confession out of Marie in a protracted catfight that destroys the saloon and Marie's criminal career.

Background: With AIP putting up $60,000 and the title, Corman filmed his third western in black and white and Superscope. Executive producer Alex Gordon was left to intervene over which actress was to get star billing. Downs, who had previously starred in John Ford's *My Darling Clementine*, expected it to go to her. Meanwhile, Castle, hired for the lead by Corman, begged to differ. In the end, the compromise reached gave Castle top billing but in the same size font as Downs. As a sop, Downs was promised star billing in another ARC film. This wouldn't occur for another two years, when she starred in Bert I Gordon's *The Amazing Colossal Man*, originally a project earmarked for Corman as *The Amazing Nth Man*. Downs' response to how things worked out is not recorded.

Verdict: An entertaining feminist slant on the traditional Western plot of the evil land-grabber holding a small town in their power. But there's enough action to keep it moving along and the players manage to breathe life into their characters, with Connors scowling convincingly for most of the film. Both Castle and Downs give vigorous performances, not least in the climactic, no-holds-barred punch-up in Marie's saloon. You can't help wondering whether the above-mentioned casting rivalry added an extra dimension to their conflict. 3/5

Gunslinger (1955)

Cast: John Ireland (Cane Miro), Beverly Garland (Rose Hood), Allison Hayes (Erica Page), Martin Kingsley (Gideon Polk), Jonathan Haze (Jake Hays), Chris Alcaide (Joshua Tate), Richard Miller (Jimmy Tonto), Bruno Ve Sota (Zebelon Tabb).

Crew: Producer/Director Roger Corman, Writers Charles B Griffith, Mark Hanna, Cinematography Fred West, Music Ronald Stein, Editor Charles Gross, 77 minutes.

Story: When Texas marshal Scott Hood is murdered in the line of duty, widow Rose does the decent thing. She straps on his guns and proceeds to clean up the lawless town. This doesn't sit well with Erica Page, a local landowner who's been trying to acquire as much of the area as possible, by nefarious means, before the railroad arrives. In order to encourage the opposition to let her have her way, Erica hires Cane, a gunslinger. At first he does his job well, eliminating those standing in the way of Erica's land-grabbing, but then he falls for Rose. Torn between duty and love, Cane goes for love. When confronted by Erica, he shoots and kills her. Rose now faces a similar dilemma but, in a final showdown with Cane, duty wins out and she shoots him dead.

Background: The film marked the start of Corman's fruitful relationship with screenwriter Griffith. He'd gone to Corman with two previous scripts co-written with Mark Hanna because Corman was known as one of the few people in Hollywood who would actually look at newcomers' scripts. Aware of Griffith's ability, Corman suggested the outline of *Gunslinger*, and Griffith and Hanna delivered.

Originally scheduled to be shot at two separate Californian ranches, Griffith had the sense to scout out locations before he wrote the script. By tweaking events around the first location, he managed to save Corman time and movement to a second locale. At first Corman was impressed. He needed to get the film shot in six days before a mandatory five-day week, negotiated between the studios and the IATSE, came into effect. But then it began to rain. Heavily and constantly. The location became a mudbath, trapping trucks and equipment. The actors did their best under the conditions, but Allison Hayes finally cracked, becoming possibly the first actress to ask the immortal question: 'Roger, who do I have to fuck to get *off* this picture?' As it turned out, no one. She later fell from her horse and broke her arm. Never one to give up, Corman (with Hayes' permission) filmed a reel of close-ups before the ambulance arrived. Garland also suffered. She twisted her ankle so badly when she fell off her horse that she finished the shoot pumped full of Novocaine. The final insult was a nest of red ants that attacked Ireland and Garland while they were filming their love scene. The shoot ran to seven days. It was the only Corman film to go over schedule and he never made another western.

Verdict: The most primitive-looking of Corman's westerns (the endless mud helps), it's arguably close to looking like something by Sam Fuller. That said, this is enjoyably demented fare, with suitably intense performances from the three leads. Fred West proves himself equally capable as Floyd Crosby at meeting Corman's demands and, despite the off-screen chaos, manages to give tension and immediacy to the various confrontations. 4/5

Day The World Ended (1955)

Cast: Richard Denning (Rick), Lori Nelson (Louise Madison), Adele Jergens (Ruby), Touch (later Mike) Connors (Tony), Paul Birch (Jim Madison), Raymond Hatton (Pete), Paul Dubov (Radek), Jonathan Haze (Contaminated man), Paul Blaisdell (Mutant).

Crew: Director/Producer Roger Corman, Writer Lou Rusoff, Cinematography Jock Feindel, Music Ronald Stein, Editor Ronald Sinclair, Special Effects Paul Blaisdell, 79 minutes.

Story: Following a nuclear holocaust, Jim Madison and his daughter, Louise, survive having settled in a valley surrounded by lead-bearing hills. Here, they are unwitting hosts for five other survivors: petty crook Tony and his girlfriend Ruby, gold prospector Pete, and engineer Rick, who arrives carrying the radiation-contaminated Radek. Living in fear of radioactive rainstorms, the group eke out the limited supplies. Tony makes several attempts to usurp Jim's control but is repelled by Jim and Rick, with whom Louise begins to fall in love. Radek gradually mutates, spending more time outside until he is killed by an extremely mutated human who stalks the survivors. Jim is contaminated while trying to stop Pete from leaving the valley. Tony kills Ruby after she thwarts his attempted rape of Louise, but then Louise is abducted by the mutant. Rick rescues her as the rains come. To their relief, it is fresh water that kills the radiation-raised mutant and disperses the fallout beyond the valley. Tony tries to ambush the couple but is killed by Jim, who dies shortly afterwards. Rick and Louise leave the valley to face their future.

Background: Filmed in Bronson Canyon (see below), the crew were in sight of the Sportsman's Lodge Restaurant on Ventura Boulevard. They were allowed to film there as long as they'd cleared out by the time dinner was served. The mutant was designed by Paul Blaisdell. Blaisdell played the monster himself, although being only 5'2" didn't help the monster's stature. To this end, Blaisdell fashioned the mutant for *Day* with eyeholes cut in the mouth, so the creature's head rose a good foot above Blaisdell's. All went well until Blaisdell had to lift and carry Lori Nelson. Nelson and he had to work a move into the film where Nelson almost lunges at the creature to fend him off and ends up in a suitable lifting position. The actual carrying went smoothly until Blaisdell caught his foot in a gopher hole.

After an uncredited appearance in *Five Guns*, Corman wangled a cameo in *Day*. Despite the creature never being identified as Nelson's fiancé, the inference is there. A photograph by Nelson's bedside depicts her and her fiancé. The man beside her is Corman.

AIP put out *Day* on a double bill with *The Phantom From 10,000 Leagues*. It was part of a gambit by AIP to wangle more money out of theatres. Normally they got a flat rate against what the theatres considered second features. With the double bill AIP sold them for the same cost as a major studio single feature. At first exhibitors wanted to split the films up and pay the flat rate, but Arkoff and Nicholson stood firm. Finally, they got a booking in Detroit, Corman's home town. Despite a blizzard and a newspaper strike, Arkoff and Nicholson were undaunted. They organised a 'horror caravan' consisting of people dressed as monsters. The stunt worked and they finally started to make money.

Verdict: Day is an effective end-of-the-world movie, competently staged with atmospheric photography from Feindel. It gets bogged down in some scenes, but the disparity in the characters' natures helps keep things lively.

More interesting are the Biblical undertones that creep into the movie, Denning and Nelson as Adam and Eve, with Blaisdell's mutant (remember, it's supposed to be Nelson's old fiancé) as the serpent. And then there is Denning and Connors' parallels to Cain and Abel; the verdant area into which the survivors stumble, the Garden of Eden. Rusoff's script might become melodramatic, but Corman's belief in the whole enterprise shapes the film into something almost reassuringly mythical. 4/5

Swamp Women (1956)

aka *Swamp Diamonds, Cruel Swamp*

Cast: Carole Matthews (Lee), Touch Connors (Bob), Beverly Garland (Vera), Marie Windsor (Josie), Jil Jarmyn (Billie), Susan Cummings (Marie), Lou Place, Jonathan Haze, Ed Nelson.

Crew: Director Roger Corman, Producer Bernard Woolner, Writer David Stern, Cinematography Fred West, Music Willis Holman, Editor Ronald Sinclair, 66 minutes.

Story: Three convicted women, Josie, Billie and Vera are helped to escape by Lee, an undercover policewoman. Lee hopes the trio will lead her to wherever they hid the stolen diamonds for which they're doing time. The women trek down to the Louisiana bayous. There they hijack a boat from a party led by Bob, a geologist. The women overpower the party, shooting Bob's guide. With Bob unconscious, they throw his girlfriend, Marie, over the side. Lee tries to protect Bob from the voracious trio while retaining her cover. This causes bickering from all concerned, particularly Bob, who's still fairly hacked off about Marie being 'gator bait. After much badinage, they recover the diamonds, only for Vera to snatch them and hide up a tree with the guns. Planning to pick off the others, she is mildly surprised when Josie gets her with a spear. Meanwhile, Lee frees Bob and together they overpower Josie and Billie.

Background: Swamp Women was filmed in Louisiana under contract from the Woolner brothers. They owned a circuit of drive-ins around New Orleans and this sort of deal was valuable to ensure that other pictures gained distribution around the same circuit. As with *Gunslinger*, the cast suffered for Corman's art. Haze, doubling as usual, acted as stunt coordinator. The actors, as was customary on Corman's often non-union movies, did their own stunts. Beverly Garland had to plummet from a tree after she'd been 'speared'. Poised about twenty feet above the swamp, Corman convinced her to take the dive. Fortunately, there was someone there to catch her, or the fall may have done for her. Afterwards, Corman's praise was typically disconcerting: 'You're the best stuntwoman I've ever worked with', he told her.

Verdict: Great title, not-so-great movie. The leading ladies give wonderfully tough performances, but the predictable plot and clichéd script don't really give them very far to go. Corman manages to work in some tired-looking Mardi Gras footage to pad out the running time. 2/5

Not Of This Earth (1956)

Cast: Paul Birch (Paul Johnson/Alien), Beverly Garland (Nadine Story), Morgan Jones (Harry Sherbourne), William Roerick (Dr Rochelle), Dick Miller (Joe Piper), Pat Flynn (Officer Simmons), Jonathan Haze (Jeremy Perrin), Ann Carol (Woman from Davanna).

Crew: Producer/Director Roger Corman, Writers Charles B Griffith, Mark Hanna, Cinematography John Mescall, Music Ronald Stein, Editor Charles Gross Jr. Special Effects Paul Blaisdell, 67 minutes.

Story: The planet Davanna is dying from a war that is evaporating its inhabitants' blood. An emissary is sent to Earth to collect fresh supplies. Under the name Paul Johnson, his dark glasses hide his mind-frazzling eyes. He hypnotises Dr Rochelle into finding a cure and Nurse Nadine into giving him regular blood transfusions. Nadine's policeman boyfriend, Harry, becomes increasingly suspicious of Johnson and his chauffeur, ex-con Perrin, but it's Nadine and Perrin who discover Johnson's matter-transmitter, which provides transport between Davanna and Earth. When a blood-deprived Davannan woman arrives, Johnson accidentally gives her rabid blood from one of Rochelle's experiments. Summoned to the hospital where she has died, Harry sees her eyes and his suspicions are confirmed. He's too late to stop Johnson killing Rochelle and Perrin, but he does save Nadine. In the ensuing car chase, Harry turns on his siren. Disoriented by the racket, Johnson crashes and dies. At his burial, Nadine and Harry encounter a stranger wearing dark glasses…

Background: Here, for the first time, Corman's 'outsider' theme is combined with that of problematic vision – as with men such as Usher and Xavier, Johnson must conceal his eyes in order to conceal his true vision. Indeed, it was Johnson's eyes that caused the biggest problem on set. Birch, not known for his sobriety, had to wear the lenses during much of the filming. Corman allowed Birch to sit around for ages between takes with the lenses still in. When Birch had to take the lenses out because of the discomfort, he realised he could barely see straight; he and Corman exchanged words. In fact, they squared off outside the house where they were filming. The fight didn't come to anything, but Birch walked off the set, which meant a stand-in had to replace him for some scenes. Fortunately, Birch had completed the most important scenes and the stand-in is the right height and build, which means that *Not* never degenerates into *Plan 9 From Outer Space.*

Verdict: The forerunner to Corman's 'comedy/horror trilogy', *Not* manages to mix some staggeringly black humour into its standard alien invasion plot: Rochelle's death by Johnson's jellyfish-monster, the transfusion of rabid blood – in the Eighties this sort of thing would become the province of the terminally-crap Troma Studios (*Class Of Nuke 'Em High*, *The Toxic Avenger*) but Corman brushes this stuff off with incredible ease. In this, he is aided by *Bride Of Frankenstein*'s cinematographer, Mescall, who turns in impressively sombre monochrome footage. 4/5

It Conquered The World (1956)

aka *It Conquered The Earth*

Cast: Peter Graves (Paul Nelson), Beverly Garland (Claire Anderson), Lee Van Cleef (Tom Anderson), Sally Fraser (Joan Nelson), Russ Bender (Patrick), Jonathan Haze (Manuel Ortiz), Richard Miller (Neil), Karen Kadler (Ellen Peters), Charles B Griffith (Pete Shelton), Paul Blaisdell (It).

Crew : Producer/Director Roger Corman, Writers Lou Rusoff, (uncredited) Charles B Griffith, Cinematography Fred West, Music Ronald Stein, Editor Ronald Sinclair, Special Effects Paul Blaisdell, 68 minutes.

Story: No one believes Dr Tom Anderson when he begs the military not to launch their latest satellite for fear of attracting unwanted extraterrestrial attention. Three months after the launch, his friend and head of the project Paul Nelson is equally dubious when Anderson claims to be in communication with Venus. Anderson's wife, Claire, fears for his sanity. But he's right and the satellite returns to earth with a Venusian stowaway. Using Anderson as its intermediary, it promises the human race a new age of reason, which unfortunately means mental enslavement. By the time Nelson realises that Anderson's telling the truth, it's too late. The Venusian has taken over key military, satellite and law enforcement personnel. He also controls Joan, Nelson's wife. Nelson kills Joan and confronts Anderson, convincing him that the Venusian will destroy the human race. Meanwhile, Claire, determined to save her husband, pursues the monster. It kills her and half the army before being annihilated by Anderson, who dies in the attempt.

Background: Corman originally designed the monster logically. Too logically, it turned out. Drawing on his background in engineering and physics, he reasoned a creature coming from Venus' heavy gravity field would have to be low to the ground. Blaisdell thus designed *It* as a rather squat creature. Preparing to shoot the showdown between Beverly Garland and *It*, Garland towered over the creature. 'So, you've come to conquer the world, have you? Take that!' she said, and kicked it in the head. Blaisdell immediately rebuilt the creature to be ten foot high. Heavy gravity or not, Corman had learned the first rule of creature features: Always make the monster bigger than your leading lady.

The creature, nicknamed Beulah, by Blaisdell, suffered further indignities. On the first day of shooting, the grips trampled its arms so that the mechanical controls stopped working. Blaisdell had to work the arms manually from inside, but, rather than the subtle movements it had originally performed, Beulah could only waggle her arms around ineffectually. At the film's finale, where Van Cleef takes a blowtorch to Beulah's eye, Blaisdell was again inside, this time with a grease gun full of chocolate syrup to simulate blood. When the time came to 'fire' the syrup, it had hardened inside the nozzle. Blaisdell had to put so much pressure on it to clear the blockage the syrup backfired on him and covered half the crew, including Corman.

Verdict: Despite the monster from another world scenario, the place where *It* is arguably strongest is the portrayal of a marriage sliding into collapse, with Garland discussing the wobbly, rather sweet, evil Venusian and its mind-controlling bat mites as if it were some two-bit trailer-park trash. Corman exploits his limited locations very well, Bronson Canyon being a prime example (used by everyone from John Ford for *The Searchers* to Wim Wenders' for *The End Of Violence*). While not quite Don Siegel's *Invasion Of The Bodysnatchers* (which also used Bronson Canyon), *It* does manage to be a first-rate exploitation of that movie's central idea. 4/5

Attack of the Crab Monsters (1957)

Cast: Richard Garland (Dale Drewer), Pamela Duncan (Martha Hunter), Russell Johnson (Hank Chapman), Leslie Bradley (Karl Weigand), Mel Welles (Jules Deveroux), Richard Cutting (Jim Carson), Beach Dickerson (Ron Fellows and The Crab), Tony Miller (Stan Sommers), Ed Nelson (Quinlin and The Crab), Charles B Griffith (Tate).

Crew: Producer/Director Roger Corman, Writer Charles B Griffith, Cinematography Floyd Crosby, Music Ronald Stein, Editor Charles Gross Jr. 62 minutes.

Story: Following the disappearance of a scientific expedition from a small Pacific island, Professor Weigand's team arrives to search for them. Located near an A-bomb test site, the island is shrinking rapidly from frequent earthquakes and landslides. The team finds journals written by McLane, head of the first expedition, which tell of wildlife mutated by A-bomb radiation. That night, team-members Martha and Jim hear McLane's disembodied voice calling them. Following the voice, Jim falls into a newly-opened pit. An unseen creature attacks Martha and her fiancé, Dale, and smashes the radio. Now Jim's voice calls to them. Others disappear.

Their voices lure the survivors underground where they find their attackers are gigantic crabs who absorb the consciousnesses of their victims; their burrowing causes the landslides. The team fights back, losing Weigand and destroying all but one crab. It attacks them on the last outcrop of the island where engineer Hank sacrifices himself to electrocute it, leaving Martha and Dale to await rescue.

Background: The crab, built by an effects team, was fifteen foot wide and made of papier mâché. Beach Dickerson's innocent enquiry 'How's it going to work?' elicited the Corman response of forcing Dickerson and Ed Nelson inside the creature and getting them to move it around. The claws were operated by piano wire, with a little assistance from the crew outside.

Charles Griffith made a similar mistake. He was so blown away by seeing some of Jacques Cousteau's underwater photography, he offered to direct the underwater sequences of *Crab Monsters* for $100. Corman jumped at the chance. It was only weeks later when Corman rang Griffith to say that the actors were on their way round for their scuba-diving lessons that Griffith realised he had to start learning himself. Thanks to Jonathan Haze, who was bringing the scuba gear, Griffith managed to get a crash course before the actors arrived.

Verdict: Yes, attack they do. Or rather one does, given that all the others are conveniently buried in a landslide early on. That said, Corman wanted action in every scene and Griffith nearly delivers. The monsters look endearingly dim and the character touches (such as Welles' fruity French accent) enliven the proceedings during the slower scenes of people wandering around caves, talking to disembodied voices. Still the king of exploitation movie titles (along with *Bloodsucking Freaks) Attack* deserves to endure for the sheer delirium of the whole enterprise and evidence of a director finally finding his forte. 5/5

She-Gods Of Shark Reef (1957)

aka *Shark Reef*

Cast: Don Durant (Lee), Bill Cord (Chris), Lisa Montell (Mahia), Jeanne Gerson (Dua), Carol Lindsay (Hula Dancer).

Crew: Director Roger Corman, Producer Ludwig H Gerber, Writers Robert Hill, Victor Stoloff, Cinematography Floyd Crosby, Music Ronald Stein, Editor Frank Sullivan, 63 minutes.

Story: Lee's Hawaiian playboy lifestyle needs cash to keep functioning. His plan to become a gun-runner goes awry when he kills the nightwatchman who catches him stealing the necessary guns. Lee gets Chris, his honest brother, to aid his escape from the island. As they head for a distant island, a storm sinks their boat. They are rescued at the last minute by the island's women and Lee and Chris soon realise they are the only men there. The women work as pearl-divers under stern matriarch, Dua, and their deity, a stone god beneath the reef's waters who demands human sacrifices. Lee soon becomes restless, but Chris wants to stay with his new love, Mahia. One night, Lee steals some pearls and flees. Chris follows and they fight. Lee falls overboard near the god and sharks get him. Adding to Chris' woes, Dua is about to sacrifice Mahia. Fortunately, he rescues her at the last minute and they sail away together.

Background: Due a vacation after juggling so many projects, Corman did the next best thing and set up a pair of deals that allowed him to film in Hawaii for a month. The first was *She-Gods Of Shark Reef.* For this, Corman was approached by Ludwig Gerber, a lawyer wanting to be a movie producer. Corman mentioned the deal to Arkoff and Nicholson and, in true AIP style, they asked him to shoot another picture in Hawaii immediately afterwards. This way, the two productions could share the same overheads for transportation and equipment, thus dramatically cutting the costs of each picture. Both pictures were brought in for under $100,000 each. Corman managed to cut costs further by getting cut-rate rooms at the Cocoa Palms Hotel so long as he credited the hotel in the pictures.

Although supposedly set in the South Pacific, *She-Gods* was mainly filmed on the Hawaiian island of Kauai, a popular location for Hollywood film-makers looking for tropical scenery without travelling to the ends of the earth. *She-Gods* sat on the shelf for nearly two years until Gerber took it to AIP. They released it on an unlikely double bill with the equally poor *Night Of The Blood Beast*, where an astronaut ends up impregnated with alien embryos. Ronald Stein is quoted as saying that he wrote sixty minutes' worth of music for *She-Gods* 'because it *needed* sixty minutes of music to save it.'

Verdict: As was often the case with AIP's product, the poster is the best thing about *She-Gods.* With a plot as dodgy as the rubbery-looking shark, it's left to the attractive Hawaiian scenery (nicely photographed by Crosby) to save the day. As to the she-gods... well, we're still waiting for them. Perhaps their boat sank. 1/5

Naked Paradise (1957)

aka *Thunder Over Hawaii*

Cast: Richard Denning (Duke), Beverly Garland (Max), Lisa Montell (Keena), Leslie Bradley (Zac), Richard Miller (Mitch), Jonathan Haze (Stony), Roger Corman (Plantation administrator), Samuel Z Arkoff (Plantation owner).

Crew: Producer/Director Roger Corman, Writers Charles B Griffith, Mark Hanna, Cinematography Floyd Crosby, Music Ronald Stein, Editor Charles Gross Jr. 68 minutes.

Story: Zac Cotton and his henchmen, Mitch and Stony, are desperate. Their payroll heist ends in murder, meaning they have to flee the island, pronto. But their getaway boat is sunk by a violent storm, forcing them to charter straight-arrow Duke Bradley's boat. As the storm continues to stall their escape, Duke rumbles them and falls for Cotton's mistress, Max. She reciprocates. Cotton is further irked by Mitch and Stony romancing local women. It gets worse. Mitch kills his girl's current boyfriend. Cotton kills Stony's girlfriend and then has to kill the protesting Stony. Max and Duke try to escape Cotton's rage, but Cotton captures Max, forcing Duke to surrender. In the final showdown, Duke wins by pushing Cotton onto the boat's propeller.

Background: At the time of making *She-Gods* and *Naked Paradise*, Corman was dating Beverly Garland. Despite the romantic setting, their relationship didn't flourish as Corman was working almost solidly while they were there. Also on the island were Arkoff and Nicholson, who'd decided to take a break and brought their families on holiday. Ever one to save money where possible, Corman roped in Arkoff to play the plantation owner. He only had one line: 'It's been a good harvest, and the money is in the safe', but it was key to the film's plot. Saving himself another actor, Corman cast himself as the plantation administrator, stabbed to death by Haze.

By another piece of fortuitous planning, Corman scheduled the film's shoot around one of the regular plantation fires (set by the sugar cane growers to clear out stubble and force the sap up into the sugarcane). Filming the fire gave the movie a sense of spectacle that the $100,000 budget would never have run to otherwise.

Verdict: *Naked Paradise* had its title changed to *Thunder Over Hawaii*, to make it sound more action packed. The film itself certainly is, with multiple killings and man-sized action all round, which help to cover up the fact that the script is a mess. Griffith was drafted in to complete it when R Wright Campbell was unable to finish, and he would use virtually the same script for *Creature From The Haunted Sea*, when it was needed in a hurry. 3/5

Carnival Rock (1957)

Cast: Susan Cabot (Natalie Cook), Brian Hutton (Stanley), David J Stewart (Christy Christakos), Dick Miller (Benny), Iris Adrian (Celia), Jonathan Haze (Max), Ed Nelson (Cannon), Chris Alcaide (Slug), Horace Logan (M C), Frankie Ray (Billy), Dorothy Neumann (Clara), The Platters, David Houston, Bob Luman, The Blockbusters.

Crew: Producer/Director Roger Corman, Writer Leo Lieberman, Cinematography Floyd Crosby, Music Walter Greene, Buck Ram, Editor Charles Gross Jr. Production Design Robert Kinoshita, 75 minutes.

Story: Christy runs a rock 'n' roll club on the Carnival Pier. Despite his debts, he ignores the advice of Benny, his right-hand man, and continues to pursue teen sensation Natalie, the club's singer. However, Natalie loves Stanley, who will stop at nothing to give her the best that life can offer. In a desperate gambling attempt to win money to escape his creditors, Christy loses the club to Stanley. Stanley lets Christy stay on as the Carnival Comic, a baggy-pants clown. Under Stanley's management, the club booms. On the eve of the couple's wedding, Stanley begs Benny to take Christy away but it's too late. Christy abducts Natalie and sets fire to the club. Both are rescued and a tearful Stanley refuses to press charges. Christy leaves the carnival with Benny.

Background: There was a great amount of excitement about getting David Stewart for the film. He'd recently been showered with plaudits for his performance on stage in Tennessee Williams' *Camino Real*. What no one knew was that he was a method actor and needed to experience the emotions that he was portraying on screen. Of all the other actors, Dick Miller seemed to come out the worst. In one scene, Stewart had to slap him. In the first take, Stewart really slapped him. Miller protested, explaining that the camera set-up meant that Stewart could miss him by a mile and it would still look like he'd been hit. Unfortunately, Stewart couldn't work like that. After a few failed attempts by Stewart to pull the punch, Corman persuaded Miller to take the slap. According to Miller, his ears rang for the next six months. For the scene where Christy has a heart attack after finding out Natalie is going to marry Stanley, Stewart handed Jonathan Haze a pin and asked him to stick it in his leg. After the scene was over, they had to extract the pin with a pair of pliers.

Verdict: The storyline is secondary to the prime importance of giving teenage audiences what they really came to see – hot rock 'n' roll, including a number from The Platters – rather than the slightly creepy tale of a fifty-year-old man lusting after teen flesh and going insane in the process. No one does solid and reliable like Dick Miller, while David J Stewart makes a meal of the big broken-hearted clown, Pagliac…er, Christy, his Greek accent drifting leisurely around the Mediterranean coast. Susan Cabot is indeed a star turn, belting out some of the movie's numbers and sobbing a lot in between. Its message, if there is one, seems to be that hey, teens have problems too. 2/5

Sorority Girl (1957)

aka *The Bad One*, *Sorority House*

Cast: Susan Cabot (Sabra Tanner), Dick Miller (Mort), Barboura O'Neill (Rita Joyce), June Kenny (Tina), Barbara Crane (Billie Marshall), Fay Barker (Mrs Tanner), Jeane Wood (Mrs Fessenden).

Crew: Producer/Director Roger Corman, Writers Ed Waters, Leo Lieberman, Cinematography Monroe P Askins, Music Ronald Stein, Editor Charles Gross Jr. 60 minutes.

Story: To claim her father's inheritance, Sabra Tanner must graduate from college. She vents her anger about this situation on her sorority sisters, especially passive Billie, whom she beats on frequently. Student president candidate Rita threatens to report Sabra's bullying to the Dean. Discovering Rita's father is in jail, Sabra blackmails her. Her plan to ruin Rita's election chances grows when she finds that sorority sister Tina is pregnant. Sabra gets Tina to blackmail Mort, Rita's campaign manager, by threatening to reveal him as the father. But Mort won't bite and gets Tina to retract the claim. When Tina attempts suicide, Mort rescues her and she reveals Sabra's plan to him. They get Rita to tell all to the sorority and the sisters expel Sabra.

Background: Corman never felt entirely comfortable directing actors, and many of his cast would recall that they were left to 'get on with it'. This isn't to suggest that Corman didn't care, but rather that he had confidence in actors to do the job they were hired to do. After all, they were the actors, he was the director; he had the entire film to take care of. But an incident with Susan Cabot on *Sorority Girl* made him realise that his directing could benefit from knowing more about the acting process. To this end, Corman enrolled in Jeff Corey's acting class. He only wanted to observe, but Corey didn't work like that. So Corman took acting classes for the next couple of years. While the quality of his films remained variable, his direction of actors improved. Although still confident they'd get the job done, the direction in films such as *Bucket of Blood* and the Poe cycle demonstrate Corman had become far more sensitive to what it takes to get the best from performers. The classes also widened his contacts, at Corey's classes he first met Robert Towne (later to write *Chinatown*) and, more importantly, Jack Nicholson.

Verdict: Sorority Girl is a step up from *Carnival Rock*, although the script never rises much above potboiler level. Cabot gives an excellent performance as the screwed-up wannabe-rich girl; all seething resentment and large, watery eyes, she still retains our sympathy. 4/5

Rock All Night (1957)

Cast: Dick Miller (Shorty), Abby Dalton (Julie), Robin Morse (Al), Richard Cutting (Steve), Bruno Ve Sota (Charlie), Chris Alcaide (Angie), Mel Welles (Sir Bop), Barboura Morris (Syl), Clegg Hoyt (Marty), Russell Johnson (Jigger), Jonathan Haze (Joey), Richard Karlan (Jerry), Jack DeWitt (Bartender), Beach Dickerson (The Kid), Ed Nelson (Pete), The Platters, The Blockbusters.

Crew: Producer/Director Roger Corman, Writer Charles B Griffith, From the teleplay *The Little Guy* by David P Harmon, Cinematography Floyd Crosby, Music Buck Ram, Editor Frank Sullivan, Art Director Robert Kinoshita, 62 minutes.

Story: Shorty is a little guy with a big chip on his shoulder. One night, he is ejected from one club and goes to another, the Cloud Nine. There, a new singer, Julie, struggles with stage fright. Despite reassurance from her hip-talking agent, Sir Bop, and Al, Cloud Nine's owner, Julie performs badly. Matters worsen when two of the club's drinkers, Jigger and Joey, are revealed to have committed robbery and murder earlier that night. Holding everyone at gunpoint, Jigger forces Julie to sing to allay the suspicions of the cops. This time, her performance is excellent, but the cops still surround the place. The desperate pair take Julie and another girl as hostages. Despite the presence of several tough guys in the club, only Shorty steps in, overpowering Jigger and forcing Joey's surrender. The cops take them away. Julie quits and leaves with Shorty.

Background: Rock All Night grew out of a standing set, and the chance to feature The Platters, a group who'd already had chart success with songs such as 'The Great Pretender' and 'Only You'. The catch was that they would be going on tour in just over two weeks. Corman remembered seeing a TV drama called *The Little Guy* set in a bar. He thought that changing the setting to a rock 'n' roll club, the story would fit around The Platters. He bought the rights to the show and set Charles Griffith to work. Unfortunately, two days before filming began, The Platters' schedule altered and Corman was told they'd only be available for a day. So Griffith now had two days to rewrite the entire script, removing virtually all references to the group and padding out the story with other characters.

Welles' character was originally written for 'Lord' Buckley, a popular comedian who used to deliver bizarre monologues in hip talk while pretending to be an English lord. Welles wrote material for him and, when Buckley disappeared before shooting began, Welles stepped into the role. Corman was concerned the audiences might be alienated by the amount of hipster slang in the film so, to counter this, Welles wrote *The Hiptionary*. Five million copies of this glossary were sent out with the prints of the film.

Verdict: Exercising the same disparate-characters-under-stress scenario that had played effectively in *Day The World Ended, Rock All Night* manages to crank up some tension. The Platters lip-synch a couple of numbers, which Corman enhances with a few judicious crane-shots (a first for him) and The Blockbusters manage to be as average as they were in *Carnival Rock*. But it's Dick Miller's film and, after a succession of supporting roles, it's refreshing to see him with something he can really get his teeth into. 3/5

Teenage Doll (1957)

aka *The Young Rebels*

Cast: June Kenney (Barbara Bonney), Fay Spain (Helen), John Brinkley (Eddie Rand), Collette Jackson (May), Barbara Wilson (Betty), Ziva Rodan (Squirrel), Sandy Smith (Lorrie), Barboura Morris (Janet), Richard Devon (Dunston), Jay Sayer (Wally), Richard Cutting (Phil Kern), Dorothy Neumann (Estelle Bonney), Ed Nelson (Dutch, Blindman), Bruno Ve Sota (Drunk), Damian O'Flynn (Harold Bonney).

Crew: Producer/Director Roger Corman, Writer Charles B Griffith, Cinematography Floyd Crosby, Music Walter Greene, Editor Charles Gross Jr. Art Director Robert Kinoshita, 67 minutes.

Story: Quarrelling over the affections of Vandals gang leader, Eddie, bad little rich girl Barbara kills Nan in self-defense. Nan's gang sisters, The Black Widows, discover the body and swear vengeance. Their leader, Helen, decides to bribe Eddie into handing Barbara over to the cops. The girls scrape the necessary money together, giving us glimpses of their unhappy home lives. Barbara's is no better. After arguing with her authoritarian father, she seeks protection from the Widows at Eddie's hideout. Reluctantly, Eddie rallies the Vandals against the Widows and their male counterparts, the Tarantulas. The ensuing fight ends with the gangs getting busted by the cops. Eddie and Barbara escape, still pursued by the Widows. A hobo who witnessed Barbara and Nan's fight corroborates Barbara's story and she stops running. Handing herself over to the cops, two of the Widows go with her.

Background: The last of the teen-themed quartet that Corman dashed out in 1957, this one took ten days, plus the weekend that Charles B Griffith took to rewrite it because the censors rejected the entire original script. Part of the problem was the Hays Office's objection to Griffith's invented weapon, the Potato Grenade – a spud studded with razor blades with a peeler as a handle. Griffith was particularly unhappy with the ending, resorted to 'because we couldn't figure out what the hell we could get away with.' The film certainly tried to play up its concerned citizen credentials, with a press pack suggesting 'juvenile panel discussions' and an anti-delinquency prologue added to the movie to divert claims of exploitation.

During the shooting of house exteriors, a next-door neighbour turned on her sprinklers in an attempt to extort money from Corman. Corman sent an assistant to ask her if she could turn them up as the water added a nice effect. She turned them off.

Verdict: Despite tough talk and method moments, *Teenage Doll* isn't helped by the alteration of its central plotting. Anyone wondering why the Widows don't just kill Barbara has to look no further than the Hays Office. That said, everyone acts their socks off, particularly Brinkley and Spain, who gets to deliver one of the most withering put-down speeches ever committed to celluloid. 4/5

The Undead (1957)

Cast: Pamela Duncan (Diana Love/Helene), Richard Garland (Pendragon), Allison Hayes (Livia), Val Dufour (Quintus), Mel Welles (Smolkin), Dorothy Neumann (Meg-Maud), Billy Barty (Imp), Bruno Ve Sota (Scroop), Aaron Saxon (Gobbo), Richard Devon (Satan), Dick Miller (Leper).

Crew: Director/Producer Roger Corman, Writers Charles B Griffith, Mark Hanna, Cinematography William Sickner, Music Ronald Stein, Editor Frank Sullivan, 71 minutes.

Story: To prove the existence of reincarnation, Quintus hypnotically regresses Diana, a prostitute. The experiment takes her back to the Middle Ages where she was Helene, a woman wrongly sentenced to be beheaded for witchcraft. In jail, Helene hears Diana's voice exhorting her to escape, which she does. Meanwhile, Helene's suitor, Pendragon, is trying to free her. They are both unaware that her arrest was caused by Helene's rival, a true witch named Livia. While Helene is smuggled to the house of white witch Meg-Maud, Livia makes plans to sacrifice Helene at the witches' Sabbath. Realising that Diana's intrusion has altered history and Helene's survival will negate her later lives, Quintus regresses himself to resolve the situation. Breaking up the Sabbath gathering, he explains everything to Helene. Hearing her future selves, Helene returns to the headman's block. Diana awakes, but Helene's death leaves Quintus no way to return from the past.

Background: Corman's first horror since *Attack Of The Crab Monsters* was almost accidental. *The Undead* was conceived as a quickie cash-in on the success of Morey Bernstein's reincarnation-friendly book *The Search For Bridey Murphy*. The film was originally titled *The Trance Of Diana Love* but when the Murphy spin-off movie (directed by Noel Langley) bombed, Corman retitled the film. It had originally been scripted by Griffith with all the Middle Ages parts voiced in iambic pentameter. These also went, much to the disappointment of the actors. The only echo of this can be found in the bust of Shakespeare overlooking Quintus and the professor and the occasional hint to *A Midsummer Night's Dream* that slips through.

Here, as with the teen movies, a particular group are constructed as outsiders on the fringes of society: here the witches, with their own hierarchical community.

Verdict: *The Undead* took ten days to shoot and $70,000 to make, and there are times when it shows. Never one to worry about niggling details, Corman's corner-cutting almost reduces the film to self-parody on occasions, such as continuity errors with the professor's glasses and in Dick Miller's fresh-faced leper (the result of filming the make-up only in a master shot). The film has plenty of ideas and, except for the two rather wooden romantic leads, good performances with both Allison Hayes' and Dorothy Neumann's witches bringing life to the film each time they appear. But its cost and quickness result in *The Undead* looking like a TV broadcast from some long-abandoned studio. In reality, it was an abandoned supermarket. 4/5

War Of the Satellites (1957)

Cast: Dick Miller (Dave Boyer), Susan Cabot (Sybil Carrington), Richard Devon (Dr Pol Von Ponder), Eric Sinclair (Dr Lazar), Michael Fox (Jason Ibn Akad), Robert Shayne (Colonel Hodgkiss), Bruno Ve Sota (M Lemoine), John Brinkley, Beach Dickerson (Crewmen), Roger Corman (Ground controller).

Crew: Producer/Director Roger Corman, Writers Lawrence Louis Goldman, (story) Irving Block, Jack Rabin, Cinematography Floyd Crosby, Music Walter Greene, Editor Irene Morra, Art Director Daniel Haller, Special Effects Jack Rabin, Irving Block, Louis DeWitt, 66 minutes.

Story: Aliens attempting to stop humans exploring space blow up every satellite launched by the United Nations Rocket Operation. They emphasize their warnings by killing UNRO chief Dr Von Ponder. His death looks like the end of the project, despite pleas from Dave Boyer, Von Ponder's assistant. However, Von Ponder arrives at the meeting and UNRO goes ahead. Under his instruction, a satellite is built in space. During construction,

Boyer witnesses Von Ponder divide into two and realises an alien force is controlling his boss. He forces Dr Lazar to conduct a medical examination on Von Ponder. Von Ponder grows a heart to pass the exam but kills Lazar anyway. Discovering Von Ponder's plans to smash the satellite into an alien force field, Boyer kills both impostors and saves UNRO.

Background: The Soviets got there first. On October 4th 1957, they launched Sputnik, the first man-made satellite to orbit Earth. Almost immediately, the special effects company headed by Jack Rabin and Irving Block, approached Corman with the suggestion that he do a satellite picture to capitalise on Sputnik's topicality. Corman contacted Allied Artists' Steve Broidy, telling him that he could have a picture shot in ten days, edited in four weeks and ready for the cinemas in two to three months to capitalise on the event, and that Broidy should get his ad department working on a campaign to promote it. Broidy took him on. In fact, the film was released six months after Sputnik launched, in May 1958, on a double bill with *Attack Of The 50ft Woman*. Daniel Haller delivered a spaceship set that consisted of four arches and a flat end. That way, Corman could either have the arches close together for a short corridor, after which the actors made a turn at the flat, or a long corridor, after which the actors made... ah, you guessed. As with *Naked Paradise*, Corman's cost consciousness extended to casting. Realising that he needed someone to play the flight controller at the beginning and at the end of the film, and that an actor hired to play this role, under union rules, would have to be paid for the entire shoot, he elected to play the role himself.

Verdict: Feeling more like an act of hubris than a genuine project, *Satellites*, excuse the pun, never really gets off the ground. While Corman's other sf/horror movies refuse to settle into simple black and white, here we're stuck with the standard bad aliens/good humans plot. One wonders exactly how much Corman wanted to make the film and how much he wanted to prove that he could make it in the time allotted. The biggest question is: given that bringing Von Ponder back from the dead has caused exactly what they were trying to avoid, why didn't the aliens just kill him? 2/5

The Saga Of The Viking Women And Their Voyage To The Waters Of The Great Sea Serpent (1957)

aka *The Viking Women And The Sea Serpent*, *Viking Women*, *Undersea Monster*

Cast: Abby Dalton (Desir), Susan Cabot (Enger), Brad Jackson (Vedric), June Kenney (Asmild), Richard Devon (Stark), Betsy Jones-Moreland (Thyra), Jonathan Haze (Ottar), Jay Sayer (Senja), Gary Conway (Jarl), Lynn Bernay, Sally Todd, Mike Forrest.

Crew: Producer/Director Roger Corman, Writers Louis Goldman, (story) Irving Block, Cinematography Monroe P Askins, Music Albert Glasser, Editor Ronald Sinclair, Special Effects Jack Rabin and Associates, 70 minutes.

Story: The tenth century. A community of Viking women set off to find their men, missing since a hunting expedition. Many of them are killed when their boat is caught in a whirlpool. The survivors, including Desir, their leader, and priestess Enger, are captured by the bloodthirsty Grimolt tribe. When the women refuse to be breeding stock they are sent to work in a quarry by Grimolt leader, Stark. There the women find their men captive. Desir is reunited with lover Vedric, whom Enger tries to seduce. Rebuffed, Enger goads Stark to kill the lovers. At the last minute, she suffers an attack of conscience and summons Thor to help. Thor obliges, raining deadly lightning onto the Grimolts. In the ensuing panic, the Vikings escape. Both Enger and Stark are killed. Out at sea, the Grimolts are killed by a gigantic sea serpent. It turns on the Vikings but Vedric spears it to death and the group sails home.

Background: The film that nearly killed the actors, the crew and Corman's reputation. Cabot and the other actors were nearly drowned more than once. The ship they were in was being towed by another, more modern boat. Their boat began to sink and they tried to alert the other boat. The guy piloting it had fallen asleep. They finally escaped by swimming ashore, only to find that they had to climb a sheer cliff as the incoming tide was filling up the cove.

The film was basically ruined by Block and Rabin. They had shown Corman wonderful drawings of the Vikings battling a monstrous sea serpent, promising the same thing for the screen. When it came to it, their creation fell far short of their promises. The serpent was much smaller than expected, and therefore completely out of scale with the actors. Also, the process plates filmed the serpent from an angle that Corman found impossible to match with the on-screen Viking action. In the end, he had to film the scene as darkly as possible, using the boat and its crew to obscure as much of the creature as possible. It looks much better on the poster.

Trying to fit the epic into a standard ten-day shoot didn't help. Corman shot location work at Iverson's Ranch and Bronson Canyon. In a race to get the picture completed against the odds, it was at Iverson's that he reached his all-time record for camera set-ups. Seventy-seven in one day.

Verdict: Everyone acts (and rows) very furiously while wearing carpets. What exactly was Corman thinking of with this disastrous prehistorical, pro-hysterical nonsense? The monster looks slightly less convincing than the Drashig in *Dr Who And The Carnival Of The Monsters,* which, in case you're wondering, is a Bad Thing. It's a misbegotten enterprise from the start. Like the Viking ship, the film should have sunk with all hands before it reached the screen. 1/5

Machine Gun Kelly (1958)

Cast: Charles Bronson (George 'Machine Gun' Kelly), Susan Cabot (Flo Becker), Morey Amsterdam (Michael Fandango), Jack Lambert (Howard), Wally Campo (Maize), Bob Griffin (Vito), Barboura Morris (Lynn Grayson), Richard Devon (Apple), Ted Thorp (Teddy), Mitzi McCall (Harriet), Frank De Kova (Harry), Shirley Falls (Martha), Connie Gilchrist (Ma Allstrom), Michael Fox (Clinton), Larry Thor (Drummond), George Archimbeault (Frank), Jay Sayer (Philip Ashton).

Crew: Producer/Director Roger Corman, Writer R Wright Campbell, Cinematography Floyd Crosby, Music Gerald Fried, Editor Ronald Sinclair, Art Director Daniel Haller, 84 minutes.

Story: Bootlegger George Kelly is goaded into bigger things by his ambitious wife, Flo. A tough guy with a gun, Kelly is pathologically terrified of death. A bank robbery turns into a bloodbath when he catches sight of a coffin. Kelly and Flo hide out at her mother's brothel and plan their next move. Flo talks Kelly into kidnapping the daughter of a wealthy local businessman. The kidnap goes without a hitch and all looks set for the pay-off. Unfortunately, Kelly makes the mistake of sending his henchman, Fandango to collect the ransom. Fandango has harboured a grudge since Kelly tortured him, costing him an arm. He leads the cops back to the hideout. Kelly goes to surrender, but Flo wants to shoot it out. Before she can do so, the police break in. When the cops ask Kelly why he didn't open fire, he replies, ''Cause I knew you'd kill me.'

Background: Corman's first foray into the gangster genre was loosely based on the real career of the one-time Public Enemy Number One. Kelly did indeed surrender in the same fashion and his wife, Kathryn, certainly seemed to be the Lady Macbeth character the film suggests. In real life their kidnapping victim was an oil baron not a little girl.

Charles Bronson's casting as lead was the result of studio politics. Originally Dick Miller was scheduled to play Kelly. However, screenwriter Campbell was pitching for his brother, William, and began to tailor the script to William's strengths. He made phone calls to Arkoff and Nicholson to try and queer Miller's pitch. To put an end to the wrangling, Corman, Arkoff and Nicholson went with Bronson who was paid $5000 for the part. The choice did Bronson and Corman a deal of good. The film was highly praised in Europe and ran at several film festivals. It was particularly well received in France, where the critics began to discuss Corman as a serious director, including examinations of his work in *Cahiers Du Cinéma*. While Corman himself was starting to take his film-making more seriously, he wasn't blind to its constraints. Rather than an artist, he still considered himself a good craftsman in a low-budget world.

Verdict: Bronson as Kelly manages to convey both the gun-wielding bravado and the emasculating weakness of one of the more complex screen gangsters. He's more than competently matched by Cabot, who gives her best Corman performance here as Kelly's manipulative wife. While Haller's sets look cheap and cheerful, they capture the period, and Crosby, as ever, backs up Corman's rapidly-paced action scenes with an almost ceaselessly roving camera. 5/5

I, Mobster (1958)

aka *The Mobster*

Cast: Steve Cochran (Joe Sante), Lita Milan (Teresa Porter), Robert Strauss (Black Frankie Udino), Celia Lovsky (Mrs Sante), Lili St Cyr (Herself), John Brinkley (Ernie Porter), Yvette Vickers (The Blonde), Robert Shayne (Senator), Grant Withers (Joe Moran), Frank Gerstle (District Attorney), Wally Cassell (Cherry-Nose), John Mylong (Mr Sante).

Crew: Director/Co-Producer Roger Corman, Co-producer Gene Corman, Writer Steve Fisher, Novel Joseph Hilton Smyth, Cinematography Floyd Crosby, Music Gerald Fried, Edward Alperson Jr. Editor William B Murphy, Art Director Daniel Haller, 80 minutes.

Story: Before a Senate hearing on organised crime, mobster Joe Sante takes the Fifth, but this doesn't stop the flashbacks. He recalls his rise through the mob, taking his boss, Frankie Udino, with him. The only woman Joe loves (besides his sainted mum), Teresa, is repelled by his career. After pulling off a hit (witnessed by Teresa's brother, Ernie), Joe becomes a made man. He travels the US with Frankie, extorting money from the unions. Teresa is flat-broke so Joe hires her as his bookkeeper. She witnesses Joe killing Ernie when Ernie attempts blackmail. Interrogated by the police, Teresa doesn't snitch. Instead, she realises how much she loves Joe. They become a couple. Godfather Moran tries to curtail Joe's growing power, but ends up dead. Joe becomes number one and is subpoenaed immediately. After the hearing, the mob believes Joe a liability and, following a failed ambush, Frankie shoots him dead in front of Teresa.

Background: Modelled on the testimony of mobsters at the early Fifties Kefauver hearings, the televised broadcasts of which had drained audiences from cinemas, *I, Mobster* was proposed by independent producer Edward Alperson. His films, released through 20th Century-Fox, gave *Mobster* a wider distribution, but Corman never felt the movie had the psychological depth of *Machine Gun Kelly*.

Verdict: The mob clichés are out in force: poverty-stricken Little Italy childhood, mobster looking for a woman to replace the beloved Ma, etc. However, Corman turns it into a gripping morality tale. 3/5

Teenage Caveman (1958)

aka *Prehistoric World, Out Of The Darkness*

Cast: Robert Vaughn (The Boy), Leslie Bradley (Symbol Maker), Darrah Marshall (The Maiden), Frank De Kova (The Villain), Robert Shayne (Keeper Of The Gifts), Ed Nelson (Tribe member), Beach Dickerson (The Fair-Haired Boy/Tom-Tom Player/The Man From The Burning Plains/ Ferocious Bear).

Crew: Producer/Director Roger Corman, Writer R Wright Campbell, Cinematography Floyd Crosby, Music Al Glasser, Editor Irene Morra, 65 minutes.

Story: The boy lives with his primitive, superstitious tribe in a desolate land. The land across the river is verdant but taboo, home of an evil god. When the boy's father is wounded in a hunting accident, the boy takes the opportunity to lead a small group across the river. When one of them dies in quicksand, the others flee home. The boy remains, later dragged back by his recovered father. The people of the tribe demand the boy's death, but eventually bow to his father's request that he is sent to Coventry until he becomes a man. The initiation passes and, even though the boy marries, he still dreams of the land across the river. Sneaking back, he fights off some stock-footage dinosaurs before meeting the evil god. It turns out to be an old man, dressed to look frightening. As the two talk, it emerges that the old man is dying from radiation poisoning and the tribe are survivors of a nuclear holocaust. Far from being a prehistoric world, it is the future.

Background: Basically a *Twilight Zone* episode but with Corman's usual budget-conscious bargain-hunting, *Teenage Caveman* is a neat little idea handled quite effectively. Filmed in the customary ten days at a budget of $70,000, *Teenage Caveman* was originally titled *Prehistoric World*. AIP changed the title to tie in with their other recent releases *I Was A Teenage Werewolf* and *I Was A Teenage Frankenstein*. It was a title that rankled with Corman, who always felt, with some justification, that it led critics to devalue it before even seeing the picture. It was also one of the few films he made where he admitted a little more time and money would have produced 'a genuinely good film instead of a pretty good one'.

As it was, every cent counted, Corman managed to flog yet another movie out of the familiar Bronson Canyon and Iverson Ranch locations, which function surprisingly well as a post-holocaust landscape. What was originally supposed to be a spacesuit for the old man is a lizard suit (previously used in *Night Of The Blood Beast*) that Corman got for $65. Corman-stalwart Beach Dickerson got to play three death scenes, attend his own funeral, perform stunt work and also play a killer bear (which resulted in him being beaten up by about thirty extras hired for the hunt scene). The dinosaurs themselves had first roamed the earth in *One Million Years BC* (1940).

Verdict: Despite these cheese-paring exercises, some slow scenes and several rather poor performances, the film works. Corman's pulp imagination triumphs again. Vaughn described it as 'the best-worst film of all time'. 3/5

3: Striking Out (1959-60)

'Roger, I tell you right now, we're discussing one hundred and fifty dollars worth of monster.'

Beach Dickerson.

By 1958, with his career expanding, Corman was investing in his own productions. These had included *The Cry Baby Killer*, which gave Jack Nicholson his movie debut, *Stake-Out On Dope Street,* which launched the careers of Irvin Kershner and Haskell Wexler, and *The Brain Eaters*. Directed by Corman regular Bruno Ve Sota, *Brain Eaters* plagiarised Robert Heinlein's novel *The Puppet Masters* and only avoided a lawsuit thanks to Corman's intervention.

Deciding it was time to start his own production company, Corman formed The Filmgroup in 1959. His aim was to produce films with budgets of $50,000 or less, in order to turn a profit. Many of the films, including *The Terror* and *Dementia 13* were distributed by AIP. While The Filmgroup made money every year, it never made enough and Corman had allowed the company to fade away by the mid-Sixties.

The Wasp Woman (1959)

aka *The Bee Girl*, *Insect Woman*

Cast: Susan Cabot (Janice Starlin), Fred (Anthony) Eisley (Bill Lane), Michael Mark (Eric Zinthrop), Barboura Morris (Mary Dennison), William Roerick (Arthur Cooper), Frank Gerstle (Les Hellman), Bruno Ve Sota (Night Watchman), Roy Gordon (Max Thompson), Frank Wolff (Delivery Man), Carolyn Hughes (Jean Carson), Lynn Cartwright (Maureen Reardon), Lani Mars (Nurse Warren), Roger Corman (Emergency Doctor).

Crew: Producer/Director Roger Corman, Writers Leo Gordon, (story) Kinta Zertuche, Cinematography Harry C Newman, Music Fred Katz, Editor Carlo Lodato, Art Director Daniel Haller, Make-up Grant R Keats, 73 minutes.

Story: Janice Starlin's cosmetics company is losing sales. As the face of her products, her ageing is making her products' effectiveness questionable. When eccentric Dr Zinthrop introduces her to the rejuvenating properties of wasp royal jelly, she is eager to become his first human guinea pig. Her employees, especially marketing director Bill Lane and chemist Arthur Cooper, believe Zinthrop is a conman and encourage Mary, Starlin's secretary, to dig deeper. All three are thrown when Starlin begins to grow younger. However, Zinthrop is attacked by a lab animal turned violent by the jelly. Dazed and horrified, he is run down by a car and ends up in a coma. Self-administering the drug, Starlin suffers side effects. At night she turns into a flesh-eating queen wasp, killing Cooper and the nightwatchman. Installing Zinthrop in a private room at the company, Starlin tries to get him to regain his memory and help her. But it's too late, Starlin changes again, kills Zinthrop and his nurse, and attacks Mary. Mary is only saved when Bill pushes Starlin to her death through a window.

Background: His first Filmgroup production, *Wasp* cost Corman $50,000, and was shot in about five days at a swift pace. To achieve maximum turnover, Corman filmed a camera angle that would recur in several scenes on the same set, with the actors hurriedly changing their clothes between set-ups. Trying to keep ahead of the schedule, Corman tried to film the climactic action scene in a single take. Cabot fared the worst from this. When Eisley throws a bottle of 'acid' at her, the plan was that Cabot would drop behind a desk and someone would sprinkle some liquid smoke on her mask and then she would come back up. She dropped all right, the bottle caught her full in the face but she kept on. Unfortunately they used too much liquid smoke, so by the time she crashed through the window, the two air holes in the mask had siphoned most of the smoke into her lungs. Finally someone twigged that she couldn't breath and they managed to get part of the mask off, taking a chunk of skin with it. For a further indignity, whenever she bit her victims, Cabot had to have a mouthful of chocolate syrup to pass for black-and-white blood. More amusingly, the zero-budget rejuvenation effects present us with the revelation that guinea pigs are adult rats. Presumably there's some kind of intermediate cocoon stage.

Verdict: Cooper's script manages to avoid the usual mad doctor clichés and gives both Zinthrop and Starlin welcome human frailties. While the poster portrayed a man in the grip of a gigantic wasp with Cabot's face, the film gave Cabot (whose male co-stars were mostly a good foot taller than her) a woolly wasp mask and fuzzy gloves to wear. Corman fleshed out the cast shortages by playing not just a doctor but a board member and a police legman as well. Much of Katz's score would later be recycled for *Little Shop Of Horrors*. The cast play their roles in a thoroughly urbane style, as if they had walked off the set of a sophisticated screwball comedy. 4/5

Ski Troop Attack (1960)

Cast: Michael Forest (Lieutenant Factor), Frank Wolff (Potter), Wally Campo (Ed), Richard Sinatra (Herman), Sheila Carol (Isle), Roger Corman (German soldier), Paul Rapp (Radio operator).

Crew: Producer/Director Roger Corman, Writer Charles B Griffith, Cinematography Andy Costikyan, Music Fred Katz, Editor Anthony Carras, 63 minutes.

Story: World War II. Five American soldiers are sent behind enemy lines to blow up a strategically important bridge. Making their way across the snow-covered countryside isn't easy, as German troops dog their steps and the Americans hate each other. Hiding from a German patrol in a mountain cabin, they meet its owner, Isle. They generally mistreat her in a boorish fashion. She tries to poison their food, but their leader, Lt. Factor stops her. Eventually she tries to shoot them but they kill her first. Leaving the cabin, they head off for the bridge. Isle's body is discovered by German troops and it's a running battle down to the bridge. All but Factor and his grouchy sergeant, Potter, are killed, but they do blow up the bridge and escape.

Background: No, it's not Germany. It's Deadwood, South Dakota. There was, of course, a financial consideration for shooting there. It was a right-to-work state, which allowed non-union pictures, thus lower pay and smaller crews. *Ski Troop* was a Filmgroup Picture, and the production and transportation costs were split between Corman and his brother Gene, who went along to produce another film, *Beast From Haunted Cave* (directed by Monte Hellman). The film's budgetary constrictions meant that the cast had to be able to ski. Most of the background troops were recruited from two local high school ski teams, so the film was shot on weekends and evenings after school. For the German ski troop leader, Corman signed up a German-born ski instructor from Sun Valley. Unfortunately, he broke a leg two days before filming, so Corman (with about two days' ski training under his belt) had to take the role. He wore goggles most of the time so that one of the high schoolers, who was about Corman's height, could do the long approach stuff. Corman just skied in and out of frame when necessary. Further problems emerged. It was a chase film so the snow had to be virgin. Any error on the skiers' parts meant that everyone would have to move to another location and start over. It was so cold that not even the Forestry Service was out in it. They had to store the film in the only car on set to stop it freezing. In another scene, Paul Rapp (who also served as location scout, assistant director and prop man) had to ski down a hill while pursued by Germans with machine-guns. Corman yelling 'Action!' into his bullhorn caused a small avalanche and Rapp got chased by more than just Germans.

Meanwhile, Corman was still yelling, telling the actors: 'STAY AHEAD OF THE AVALANCHE!'

Verdict: Was it all worth it? Well it made its money back at the box office (released as a double bill with *Battle Of Blood Island*) and it does have various skirmishes to liven it up, along with the bridge explosion. But the behind-the-scenes events are far more exciting than what is on screen, which is a fairly dull war flick. 2/5

A Bucket Of Blood (1959)

Cast: Dick Miller (Walter Paisley), Barboura Morris (Carla), Antony Carbone (Leonard De Santis), Julian Burton (Maxwell Brock), Ed Nelson (Art Lacroix), John Brinkley (Will), John Shaner (Oscar), Judy Bamber (Alice the awful), Myrtle Domerel (Mrs Surchart), Burt Convy (Lou Raby), Jhean Burton (Naolia), Alex Gottlieb (Singer), Bruno Ve Sota (Art Collector).

Crew: Producer/Director Roger Corman, Writer Charles B Griffith, Cinematography Jack Marquette, Music Fred Katz, Editor Anthony Carras, Art Direction Daniel Haller, 66 minutes.

Story: Simple-minded but well-meaning busboy, Walter Paisley works at The Yellow Door, a Beat café. Bullied by Leonard, his boss, Walter is fascinated by the Beats, especially poet Maxwell Brock, and Carla, whom he secretly loves. Although he lacks artistic talent, Brock's latest poem fires Walter to be creative. He buys some clay but his sculptures fail miserably. Attempting to free a cat trapped behind the wall of his apartment, he accidentally stabs it to death. Remembering Brock's poem, he covers the cat with clay and presents it to Leonard and Carla as 'Dead Cat'. Leonard agrees to display it in the café. The Beats embrace Walter as a genius. Brock eulogises him in a poem and Beat girl Naolia gives him a packet of heroin in appreciation. This exchange is seen by Lou, an undercover cop. When Lou tries to arrest him, Walter panics and kills him with a frying pan. Meanwhile, Leonard has knocked over 'Dead Cat' and discovered Walter's secret. He is aghast when informed that Walter's next sculpture is 'Murdered Man' but his secrecy is guaranteed when offered $500 for the cat. Dizzy with praise, Walter fears being forgotten and finds new victims. Hoping to stop the mayhem, Leonard gives Walter a show at the café. On the night, Walter is first rejected by Carla and then discovered by the critics, in both ways. Pursued by cops and Beats, Walter flees. Breaking down his apartment door, they discover Walter has created his masterpiece 'Hanged Man'.

Background: Made on the standing sets of AIP's *Diary Of A High School Bride* (1959), Corman had toured them with Griffith and invited him to write a script around them. That evening, they drifted through coffee houses around Sunset Strip until they came up with the storyline. Originally titled *The Yellow Door*, and promoted as *The Living Dead*, Griffith's script is a rare Hollywood attempt to represent the beatnik lifestyle as a genuine alternative culture, rather than the usual work-shy layabout clichés that were common media representation. Filmed in five days on a budget of $50,000, beating Corman's previous shooting record by a day, *Bucket* was remade in 1995 as *Dark Secrets*, with Corman as executive producer. It starred Anthony Michael Hall and neatly satirised the modern art scene instead of the Beats.

Bucket is arguably one of the first horror films to exploit black comedy to its advantage. Of course, there are predecessors, predominantly James Whale's *Bride Of Frankenstein* and *The Old Dark House*, but here it was elevated to a genre all its own. Both *Bucket* and *The Little Shop Of Horrors* revel in their nastiness while always acknowledging how stupid death, ambition, greed and other human frailties really are. Their real impact wouldn't be truly acknowledged until the explosion of horror comedies in the Eighties, the best of which, Stuart Gordon's *Re-Animator*, Dan O'Bannon's *The Return Of the Living Dead* and Peter Jackson's *Braindead*, probably the ultimate extrapolation of the theme, kept up the same uneasy balance of laughing in the mortuary.

Verdict: In *Bucket*, Corman's rep players finally get a chance to shine. Miller, Carbone, Morris and Ve Sota are all clearly enjoying themselves in this great romp. The plot never passes up the chance for a cheap gag (Brock's wonderful Ginsberg piss-take; his sandals-with-evening-wear look came about because his feet had swollen in the LA heat and he couldn't wear the shoes that wardrobe had supplied) and the gags never get in the way of a fiendishly nasty plot (inspired by Michael Curtiz's *Mystery Of The Wax Museum* and Andre De Toth's *House Of Wax*). Carbone's Leonard is a joy as he swings from bullying boss to shaky, nauseated patron, entangled in Walter's crimes by his greed for cash and desperately trying to steer Walter's 'art' away from realism. The scene where Walter unveils 'Murdered Man' and Carla coos in wonder while Leonard staggers around in the background like a man beaten senseless with horror is a classic of the genre. 5/5

The Little Shop Of Horrors (1960)

Cast: Jonathan Haze (Seymour Krelboind), Jackie Joseph (Audrey), Mel Welles (Gravis Mushnik), Dick Miller (Burson Fouch), Myrtle Vail (Winifred Krelboind), Leola Wendorff (Siddie Shiva), Jack Nicholson (Wilbur Force), John Shaner (Dr Farb), Meri Welles (Leonora Clyde), Tammy Windsor, Toby Michaels (Teenage Girls), Dody Drake (Waitress), Charles B Griffith (Thief/Voice of Audrey, Jr.).

Crew: Producer/Director Roger Corman, Writer Charles B Griffith, Cinematography Archie Dalzell, Music Fred Katz, Editor Marshall Neilan Jr. Art Director Daniel Haller, 70 minutes.

Story: Simple-minded but well-meaning Seymour Krelboind works for irascible Gravis Mushnik at his florist's shop on Skid Row alongside Audrey, his secret love. Business is poor, but Seymour presents Mushnik with an unusual plant he has grown in the hope of attracting customers. He has christened it Audrey Jr. which wins Audrey's affections. It is strange with characteristics of the Venus Flytrap. But, once displayed, it immediately draws customers. Mushnik is overjoyed, until Audrey Jr wilts. Staying after closing, Seymour discovers that Audrey Jr. thrives on blood. It begins to grow and talk, but only begs Seymour to feed it. Having 'run out of blood', Seymour goes for a walk and accidentally kills an undercover cop. Mushnik witnesses Seymour feeding Audrey Jr. with the body. Vowing to call the cops, continuing increase in trade ensures Mushnik's silence. So it continues. Each leap in Audrey Jr.'s growth comes from a body. Seymour kills his sadistic dentist and a prostitute, and Mushnik lures a burglar into the plant's maw. The plant's prodigious size draws the praise of a horticultural group and, at their award presentation, the jig is up when Audrey Jr.'s buds bloom to reveal the faces of its victims. Investigating the disappearances, the police chase Seymour but lose him. He returns to the shop and climbs into Audrey Jr. with a knife. But the next day a new flower appears…

Background: Another Corman movie about which legends abound. Here they seem to be confirmed. Corman was bet that he couldn't make a film around the standing set of a shopfront. Corman said that he didn't have a movie in mind, but if they could leave the set for a fortnight, he'd come up with something and film it in two days to boot. As always, he came through, with a little bending. He shot the stage work in two days, while screenwriter Griffith shot the exterior footage in two days and four nights. Griffith hired skid-row bums for his crew and extras at ten cents a pop. Much has been said on the fact that the script was entirely ad-libbed, not least by Griffith. But Mel Welles insists that everything was tightly scripted and that Griffith, a close friend and fan of Welles' Yiddisher comedy routines, should take full rewards for his work.

Griffith was also the voice of Audrey Jr. originally, only filling the role so that Haze had someone to time his part against, his performance worked well enough that Corman didn't bother to redub the part.

Little Shop was further elevated when it was made into a stage musical by lyricist Howard Ashman, with music by Alan Menken. In 1986, Corman signed a deal with Warner Brothers for a film of Ashman's musical. Whereas the musical had retained Griffith's unhappy ending, the film did not, vanquishing Audrey Jr. and reuniting Seymour with Audrey, Sr. Directed by Frank Oz, it starred Steve Martin.

Verdict: 'Feeeeed Meeeee!'. Cheaply made, quickly shot and very enjoyable, *The Little Shop Of Horrors*, like *A Bucket Of Blood*, is the distillation of Corman's work ethic. Indeed, plot similarities abound: the dozy underdog stumbling on something that gains him affection and recognition, the complicity of the boss in the ghastly undertakings necessary to retain the status quo, the police investigation, and the undoing and death of the hero by the very materials that brought him success. Unlike *Bucket*, Griffith's humour has no specific target here. Where that film satirized the first-person anal nature of the Beats, *Little Shop* just revels in silliness for the sake of it. Nowhere is this more apparent than in the characters' names. So much so that, when Burson Fouch is first introduced to Gravis Mushnik, he exclaims, 'Ooh, that's a good one!' Not that this makes it a lesser film. There are some deliciously dark moments, particularly when Mushnik, seeking to reassure himself that the murders will not continue, discusses Audrey Jr.'s nature with Seymour. By explaining the life cycle of the Venus Flytrap, that only feeds three times before reaching its adult size, the two characters manage to convey that Mushnik knows, that Seymour knows Mushnik knows, and that they are both horribly wrong. Nicholson's cameo as Farb's masochistic patient is an equally pleasant bonus. 5/5

The Last Woman On Earth (1960)

Cast: Antony Carbone (Harold), Betsy Jones-Moreland (Evelyn), Edward Wain (aka Robert Towne) (Martin).

Crew: Producer/Director Roger Corman, Writer Robert Towne, Cinematography Jack Marquette, Music Ronald Stein, Editor Anthony Carras, 71 minutes.

Story: Mobster Harold, Evelyn, his moll, and Harold's lawyer, Martin, are scuba-diving when the nuclear holocaust comes. Thanks to being underwater, they are the only survivors. Growing bored with looting, the love-triangle dynamic begins to kick in and the two men begin to vie for Evelyn's affections. Darwinian Martin believes that, if Harold wins, the new humans will be as equally thuggish. Evelyn eventually falls for Martin and runs off with him. Confirming Martin's viewpoint, an enraged Harold tracks them down and the two men slug it out. Harold finally kills Martin and gets the girl. A little too late, he enquires 'Will we never learn?', before they head off into the nuclear sunset.

Background: For *Last Woman* Corman headed down to Puerto Rico, mainly because of encouraging tax breaks for film-makers. During the shoot, he also produced a World War II picture, *Battle Of Blood Island*. During his stint at Jeff Corey's acting class, he had met Robert Towne. Towne was also trying to break into screenwriting and so Corman gave him the job of writing *Last Woman*. Unfortunately, Towne was a slower worker than Corman needed and the script wasn't finished before cast and crew were due to leave for Puerto Rico. In order to fit Towne's journey into the film's budget, he also hired him as an actor. Thus, Towne appeared in both *Last Woman* and *Creature From The Haunted Sea* under the pseudonym Edward Wain. In the meantime, Corman had financed a teen-rebellion flick called *The Wild Ride*, directed by UCLA graduate, Harvey Berman. When that film wrapped, the residue of the production money was returned to Corman's account, just in time to provide funds for shooting *Creature From The Ocean Floor*.

Verdict: *Last Woman* is definitely low-end Corman. Shot in two weeks, with decent location photography by Jacques Marquette, it returns to the concerns of *The Day The World Ended*. Unfortunately, this time there are no mutants to liven up the proceedings. 1/5

The Creature From The Haunted Sea (1960)

Cast: Antony Carbone (Renzo Capeto), Betsy Jones-Moreland (Marybelle Monahan), Edward Wain (aka Robert Towne) (Sparks Moran), Edmundo Rivera Alvarez (Colonel Tostada), Robert Bean (Jack), Sonya Noemi Gonzalez (Mango), Beach Dickerson (Pete Peterson, Jr).

Crew: Producer/Director Roger Corman, Director Pre-Titles Sequence Monte Hellman, Writer Charles B Griffith, Cinematography Jacques Marquette, Music Fred Katz, Editor Angela Scellars, Monster construction Beach Dickerson, Robert Bean, 60 minutes.

Story: Following the Cuban revolution, loyalists entrust the National Treasury to Renzo Capeto, a small-time hood, to take it and troops out of the country to start the counter-revolution. Sailing away, Capeto and his gang invent a sea monster with which to scare off the Cubans. What no one realises is that a real sea monster is also picking off Cubans. Several victims on, Capeto scuttles the boat, dropping the gold overboard, planning to retrieve it later. The Cubans aren't so easily dissuaded and start diving for the gold. Capeto's gang and the monster continue killing. When one of the gang is killed by the monster, suspicion falls on Capeto. The remaining Cubans decide to flee but the monster has other ideas. It launches a final assault, which only undercover agent, Sparks Moran, and his new-found love survive. The monster gets the gold.

Background: Corman was in Cuba when Fidel Castro seized power. With Corman were producers Bernard and Larry Woolner; the plan was to make a film for Cuban Color Films. The revolution changed their minds and the trio hastily returned to the US, but events provided the inspiration for *Creature*. Still in Puerto Rico after wrapping *Last Woman*, Corman decided to stay an extra week and make another movie, using the same cast. He contacted Charles Griffith for another horror comedy script. At first, Griffith blanched at the short timescale, but with some fulsome praise from Corman about the scripts for *Bucket* and *Little Shop*, he finally agreed. The script was mailed to Corman in parts and gave him a major role. Allegedly the most complex character in the film, Happy Jack Monahan, Corman stepped down and gave the role to Bean, his boom operator. Bean also played the monster, which he and Beach Dickerson knocked together out of a wetsuit covered in oilcloth, moss and Brillo pads. The head was five army helmets, with tennis balls for eyes.

Verdict: The slightest of Corman's comedy horrors. *Creature*'s humour veers between digs at the film's low budget and Moran's Frank Drebin-style voice-overs. The ramshackle monster's appearances enliven the proceedings greatly but mainly it feels that you're just watching someone's goofy holiday movies. 2/5

Atlas (1960)

Cast: Michael Forest (Atlas), Frank Wolff (Praximedes), Barboura Morris (Candia), Walter Maslow (Garnis), Christos Exarchos (Indros), Andreas Fukippides (Talectos), Theodore Dimitriou (Gallus), Miranda Kounekelaki (Ariana), Sascha Dario (Prima ballerina), Charles Griffith (Greek soldier).

Crew: Producer/Director Roger Corman, Writer/Associate Producer Charles B Griffith, Cinematography Basil Maros, Music Ronald Stein, Editor Michael Luciano, 84 minutes.

Story: The war between Thenis and Seronikos has been running for months, with no sign of either side winning. Eventually they settle on a champion from each side to do battle and settle the matter in a more economical fashion. Praximedes, Seronikos's tyrannical leader uses his wife, Candia, as bait to get Atlas to fight their corner. Atlas wins the competition, thus leaving the way clear for Praximedes to wipe out the people of Thenis. Realising he's been set up, Atlas leads a successful rebellion, killing Praximedes in single combat.

Background: Originally Corman had intended to make a film about the U-2 spyplane scandal that had erupted the previous year. Corman had backing from Nat Cohen at Anglo-Amalgamated. All he needed was the script he'd commissioned from Robert Towne. Towne was so slow that Corman decided on another tack. Joseph Levine was doing well with *Hercules*, the first Steve Reeves sword 'n' sandal epic, to which he had bought the US distribution rights. Corman thought he could do the same but film it instead. Originally a Greek producer was going to put up the money and supply hundreds of extras from the Greek army. He failed to do both, leaving Corman with a budget of $40,000 and a handful of extras. He tried to treat it like his westerns, using natural locations. He even got Griffith to rescript various scenes with dialogue that would explain why the buildings were ruins and the army only consisted of a handful of men, but it failed to convince. It was further hindered when the Greek crew went on strike halfway through filming, sending the costs 'soaring' to $70,000.

Verdict: All in all, a miserable history to a fairly miserable film. 0/5

4: Without You I Am Nothing (1960-65)

'I had been passing alone, on horseback, through a singularly dreary tract of country; and at length found myself, as the shades of evening drew on, within view of the melancholy House of Usher.'

Edgar Allan Poe, *The Fall Of The House Of Usher*

'I sometimes feel that I'm impersonating the dark unconscious of the whole human race. I know this sounds sick, but I love it.'

Vincent Price

As with many independent production companies, AIP had come under attack for exploiting sex and violence in their movies. Now seen as either innocuous or just plain camp, films such as Howard Koch's *I Was A Teenage Werewolf* and William Witney's *The Cool And The Crazy* were seen at the time as dangerous promotions of teen violence and drug use. Corman and AIP's venture to counter these accusations was the production of well-mounted adaptations of Edgar Allan Poe's classic horror stories. While the stories were taught in high schools from coast to coast, the movies, known as Corman's 'Poe Cycle', exposed their audiences to far more perverse acts than Michael Landon's track-suited lycanthrope or hopped-up teens could ever hope to achieve.

House of Usher (1960)

aka *The Fall Of The House Of Usher*

Cast: Vincent Price (Roderick Usher), Mark Damon (Philip Winthrop), Myrna Fahey (Madeline Usher), Harry Ellerbe (Bristol), Bill Borzage, Mike Jordan, Nadajan, Ruth Oklander, George Paul, David Andar, Eleanor Le Faber, Geraldine Paulette, Phil Sylvestre, John Zimeas (Ghosts).

Crew: Director/Producer Roger Corman, Writer Richard Matheson, Cinematography Floyd Crosby, Music Les Baxter, Editor Anthony Carras, Set Design Daniel Haller, Special Effects Ray Mercer, Pat Dinga. 79 minutes

Story: Philip Winthrop visits his fiancée, Madeline Usher, at her family home. It is a crumbling mansion on the edge of a stagnant tarn. Madeline's brother, Roderick, is less than welcoming and strongly against their marrying. The Usher line, he explains, is one tainted with villainy and madness and should end with them. Roderick and Madeline's cross to bear is a 'morbid acuteness of the senses' and an acute morbidity. In the family crypt, Madeline shows Winthrop the places already prepared for her and her brother. Winthrop convinces her to leave with him but, after arguing with Roderick, Madeline collapses and dies. At the funeral, Roderick sees her hand move, but inters her before Winthrop notices. Next day, the family retainer lets slip that the Usher line has a history of catalepsy. Winthrop breaks open Madeline's tomb, but her coffin is gone. Roderick confesses he heard her waking screams and moved the coffin so she couldn't be rescued. Desperately searching the house, Winthrop finds the coffin. It is empty; Madeline has escaped. Driven insane, she attacks Winthrop and kills Roderick as the house destroys itself around them. Only Winthrop escapes as the house collapses into the tarn.

Background: Corman had long wanted to film Poe's story. When Nicholson hired him to make two black-and-white horror movies on two ten-day shoots, Corman talked him into combining the budgets for one colour horror on a fifteen-day shoot. Sam Arkoff took a little more convincing. 'Where's the monster?' he asked. 'The house is the monster', Corman replied. During the shooting, Vincent Price questioned the line in his script: 'The house lives. The house breathes'. 'What does that mean?' he asked Corman.

'That's the line that allowed us to do this movie,' was Corman's response.

The film cost $270,000 to make and Corman brought it in on schedule. It was the biggest budget AIP had ever given to a single movie but their faith was rewarded, *Usher* earned them over $1 million in rentals alone. Nicholson and Arkoff were not slow in getting Corman to direct a follow-up.

Art director Daniel Haller had worked on and off with Corman since *War Of The Satellites* and his ability to make something out of almost nothing was boosted by a set design budget of $20,000. Many of the major studios allowed production companies free access to the scene docks and, for $2,500, Haller and Corman availed themselves of stock sets from Universal for *Usher*. The film's look was further aided by two fires. The first was a forest fire that had ravaged part of the Hollywood hills the previous day. Corman set up a fog machine and it's this blackened landscape that Mark Damon rides through in the film's opening. The second fire was intentional. Hearing about a barn in Orange County that was due to be demolished, Corman offered the owner $50 to burn it down and filmed the results using a two-camera set-up. The footage of the fire would be reused several times during the Poe cycle and later resurfaced at the climax of the feeble H P Lovecraft adaptation *The Shuttered Room*.

Verdict: While it is arguable that Corman never made a *great* film, *Usher*, along with *The Masque Of The Red Death* is certainly one of his greatest, and the finest of his Poe cycle. Matheson's script adds Winthrop and Madeline's romance to Poe's story, but otherwise remains notably faithful. Corman's interest with Freudian psychology is apparent, not only in Price's incestuous desire for Madeline, but in the transference of these corrupting desires onto the house itself. The leisurely 15-day shoot and bigger budget finally allowed Corman to show what he was truly capable of. Under his direction, Daniel Haller's mouldering sets, Floyd Crosby's continually searching camerawork and Price's magnificently nuanced performance come together to form a coherent whole. 5/5

The Pit And The Pendulum (1961)

Cast: Vincent Price (Nicholas Medina), John Kerr (Francis Barnard), Barbara Steele (Elizabeth Barnard Medina), Luana Anders (Catherine Medina), Antony Carbone (Dr Charles Leon), Patrick Westwood (Maximilian), Lynne Bernay (Maria), Larry Turner (Nicholas as a child), Mary Menzies (Isabella), Charles Victor (Bartolome).

Crew: Director/Producer Roger Corman, Writer Richard Matheson, Cinematography Floyd Crosby, Music Les Baxter, Editor Anthony Carras, Art Director Daniel Haller, Special Effects Pat Dinga, 85/80 minutes.

Story: 16th century Spain. Following the mysterious death of his sister, Elizabeth, Francis Barnard arrives at the castle of her husband, Nicholas Medina. Barnard also meets Medina's sister Catherine, and the family doctor, Charles Leon. It transpires that Elizabeth had become increasingly obsessed with the castle's torture chamber, a relic of the Medinas' father, Sebastian, head torturer for the Inquisition. On the eve of taking Elizabeth away from the castle, Nicholas found her dying in the chamber. Her last word: 'Sebastian.' Catherine tells Barnard that Nicholas was traumatised as a child when he witnessed Sebastian kill his brother and bury his wife alive after discovering their affair. Elizabeth's ghost seems to haunt Nicholas. He suspects she was also buried alive. Opening her coffin, his fears are confirmed. That night, Nicholas witnesses Elizabeth rise from the tomb. She pursues him to the torture chamber and his mind snaps. Elizabeth and her lover, Leon, congratulate themselves on their clever plan. However, Nicholas revives as Sebastian. Locking Elizabeth in an iron maiden, he pursues Leon into an antechamber where the pit and the pendulum await. Leon falls into the pit and dies. Intervening, Barnard is bound beneath the pendulum, a razor-sharp blade that swings down to its victim. Catherine brings help, Nicholas dies in the pit and Barnard is saved. He and Catherine lock the chamber forever, unaware that Elizabeth still lives.

Background: After *Usher*'s success, AIP were keen for Corman to direct a follow-up. Corman commissioned a treatment of *The Masque Of The Red*

Death but was also engaged in shooting *Atlas* in Greece and preparing to film *The Intruder*. So *The Pit And The Pendulum* was settled on, with another fifteen-day shoot and similar budget. Having the good sense to hold on to the set units for *Usher*, the set budget for *Pit* allowed Daniel Haller to build upon it, making *Pit*'s look much grander. Unlike *Usher*'s narrative, screenwriter Matheson had less to build on, for Poe's story is an interior monologue of a man subjected to the dreaded pit and pendulum after being wrongfully imprisoned by the Spanish Inquisition. At the last minute he is saved by the French army. Matheson thus changed the main focus to Price's character, making him similarly obsessed to Roderick Usher but this time more sinned against.

Corman used several crane set-ups for the climatic pendulum scene, often improvising the shots and then choreographing it during the editing stage. The pendulum itself was a proper working model but moved too slowly for Corman's taste, so he cut out every other frame with an optical printer making its movement twice as fast. For the longshots, a wooden model was used, but in the close-ups a razor-sharp blade was used. Actor Kerr was protected by a steel band and his chest was padded and covered with fake skin that bled as the blade tore through his shirt. Barbara Steele, whose remarkable face graced many Italian horror movies of the Sixties, was hired on the strength of her appearance in Mario Bava's *La Maschera Del Demonio* (aka *Black Sunday*).

Pit proved even more successful at the box office, taking close to $2 million in rentals. However, due to a disagreement over his director's fee, Corman's next Poe adaptation would not be made for AIP.

Verdict: Visually, *Pit* looks more impressive than *Usher*; Floyd Crosby's increasingly fluid camerawork adds a further layer of menace to the proceedings, along with the coloured gels that flood the flashback sequences with blues and purples. Unlike *Usher*, the sub-plot necessary to flesh out Poe's story doesn't sit entirely well within the film. That said, the Freudian undertones of the film are again well thought out with Price confusing his wife with his mother and then turning into his father. Where *Pit* comes into its own, however, is the frenzied action at the film's climax, which is beautifully handled, plunging us into the delirium of the dreadful antechamber and Price's vengeance. 4/5

The Intruder (1962)

aka *The Stranger*, *Shame*, *I Hate Your Guts*

Cast: William Shatner (Adam Cramer), Frank Maxwell (Tom McDaniel), Beverly Lunsford (Ella McDaniel), Robert Emhardt (Verne Shipman), Jeanne Cooper (Vi), Leo Gordon (Sam Griffin), Charles Barnes (Joey Greene), Charles Beaumont (Mr Paton), Katherine Smith (Ruth McDaniel), George Clayton Johnson (Phil West), William F Nolan (Bart Carey), Phoebe Rowe (Mrs Lambert), Bo Dodd (Sheriff), Walter Kurtz (Gramps), Ocee Ritch (Jack Allardyce).

Crew: Producer/Director Roger Corman, Writer Charles Beaumont, from his novel, Cinematography Taylor Byars, Music Herman Stein, Editor Ronald Sinclair, 84 minutes.

Story: Southern USA. Racist rabble-rouser Adam Cramer arrives in the small town of Caxton to stir up its populace against the integration of black students at the high school. It doesn't take much. The only opposition comes from Caxton's newspaper editor, Tom McDaniel, whose daughter Ella attends the school. Cramer sets about seducing Ella. On the first day of school, the black students are met by protestors but proceed. Cramer's rhetoric spurs Caxton's Klan chapter to firebomb the local black church, killing the pastor. Cramer is unaware at first, for he is taking advantage of Viv, the wife of Sam Griffin, a travelling salesman. Imprisoned for the bombing, Cramer is bailed out by the townsfolk. Griffin confronts him about Viv (who has fled) and questions his ability to control the mob. That morning, McDaniel is viciously beaten for walking the black students to school. Cramer exploits this, telling Ella her father will be killed unless she claims Joey Green, one of the black students, tried to rape her. Ella does so. Led by Cramer, the mob invade the school and, against his wishes, tie Joey to a swing. Griffin arrives and gets Ella to tell the truth. Despite Cramer's pleas, the crowd realise they have been used and disperse, leaving him powerless.

Background: Corman's most, perhaps only, personal picture. It cost $80,000 and was mostly self-financed. *The Intruder* was filmed over three weeks on location in Sikeston, East Prairie, and Charlston, Missouri, a town where Cramer's racist sentiments were readily agreed with. Apart from the leads, most of the actors and crew were from the area so authenticity was maintained. Corman hired most of the town as extras and gave them scripts that were deliberately watered down, so as to try and conceal the film's liberal message. But word leaked out and threatening phone-calls and letters became regular occurrences. Shooting the climactic scene in the school yard, Corman and his crew were forced out by the local sheriff. They only got the rest of the scene shot in another school yard thanks to his brother Gene's ability to keep the cops talking while Corman raced through the set-ups. For the final establishing shot, Corman returned to the previous school on his own as not even the cameraman would return. He made it out with the sheriff on his heels, but he got the shot.

Beaumont's 1958 novel drew its inspiration from the activities of John Kasper, a Northern rabble-rouser who had tried to sabotage school integration in Clinton, Tennessee, in 1957. While the ending is a little unconvincing, (in Beaumont's novel the National Guard have to be called in) it remains a powerful film from a clearly socially-committed director. Shatner gives the performance of his career (sorry, Trekkers) ably supported by an excellent cast. The stark black and white photography perfectly captures the sweaty, seething atmosphere of a town on the brink of mob rule. Beaumont himself plays the school principal, while fellow *Twilight Zone* writers George Clayton Johnson and William F Nolan have smaller parts.

Verdict: The Intruder won Corman the best reviews of his career, it was shown at the Venice Film festival and at Cannes. Unfortunately, audiences were not so impressed; it was his first film to make a financial loss. He partly blamed the fact that he couldn't get a proper distribution (AIP, United Artists and Allied Artists backed out; he resorted to releasing it through his own Filmgroup when Pathé Laboratories pulled out of the distribution business), but mainly he blamed himself. From then on, whenever he wanted to get his message across, he would couch it within the text of a genre that audiences would want to see. Films such as *The Wild Angels* and *The Trip* proved his point, but that doesn't make *The Intruder* any less of an important and brave film. Along with the Poe cycle, it proved that Corman wasn't merely an exploitation director but someone who could use his low-budget circumstances to produce something of lasting value. 5/5

The Premature Burial (1962)

Cast: Ray Milland (Guy Carrell), Hazel Court (Emily Gault), Richard Ney (Miles Archer), Heather Angel (Kate Carrell), Alan Napier (Dr Gideon Gault), John Dierkes (Sweeney), Dick Miller (Mole), Brendan Dillon (Minister).

Crew: Director/Producer Roger Corman, Writers Charles Beaumont, Ray Russell, Cinematography Floyd Crosby, Music Ronald Stein, Editor Ronald Sinclair, Art Director Daniel Haller, 81 minutes.

Story: Witnessing the illegal exhumation of a cataleptic, Guy Carrell's fear of premature burial becomes a full-blown obsession. He is convinced that a similar fate befell his father. Despite this, and his sister Kate's disapproval, he marries Emily, the daughter of a surgeon, Gideon Gault. However, Guy starts to believe that Gault's 'resurrectionists', Sweeney and Mole, are pursuing him. Seeking assistance, Emily summons a mutual friend, Dr Miles Archer. When Archer arrives, Guy has built, and is occupying, a premature burial-proof tomb. Later, walking with Emily, Guy is pursued by Sweeney and Mole, although Emily denies this. She forces Guy to choose between her and the tomb. He relents and destroys the tomb. That night, an intruder enters the family vault… Guy's recovery stalls when a cat is found walled up. Freeing it, Miles challenges Guy to prove his father was buried alive. Opening the vault, dad's corpse falls out on Guy, who falls into a cataleptic trance. Miles declares Guy dead and Guy experiences his own burial. Unwittingly rescued by Sweeney and Mole, Guy kills them and Gault. He arrives home to see Emily seduce Archer. Guy buries Emily alive and nearly kills Archer before Kate shoots him dead. Over the bodies, Kate tells Archer she knew Emily planned everything but thought Guy wouldn't believe her (however, she could have *tried*).

Background: After the financial failure of *The Intruder*, Corman returned to Poe. Tired of settling his fee by flipping a coin with Sam Arkoff, he took *The Premature Burial* to Pathé Laboratories, who handled much of AIP's print work and were keen to get involved in film production. To flesh out what was basically an essay by Poe on his own fear of premature burial, Corman hired Charles Beaumont and the man who had given Beaumont his major break, Ray Russell. Russell had become executive editor of *Playboy* in its formative years, creating one of the major adult markets for sf and horror writers during the Fifties. Corman originally intended to cast Vincent Price in the lead but AIP had Price in an exclusive contract so he went with Milland, his next choice. On the first day of shooting, Corman was surprised to see Arkoff and Nicholson arrive on the set. Arkoff shook Corman's hand. 'We just wanted to wish you luck,' he said. 'We're partners again.' While Corman had been busy, AIP had gone to Pathé and, using the threat of withdrawing their print work as leverage, bought the production rights to the film.

Verdict: The slightest and weakest of all of Corman's Poe adaptations, *The Premature Burial*'s strength is in Haller's art direction (particularly the foolproof tomb) as well as the hallucinatory dream sequence where Milland's obsession gains the upper hand. Its greatest failing is in casting Milland. While he turns in a decent performance, he brings none of the tortured vulnerability to the role that one could have expected from Vincent Price. 2/5

Tales Of Terror (1962)

aka *Edgar Allan Poe's Tales Of Terror*

Cast: Vincent Price (Locke/Fortunato/M Valdemar), Peter Lorre (Montresor), Basil Rathbone (Mr Carmichael), Debra Paget (Helene), Joyce Jameson (Annabel), Maggie Pierce (Lenora), Leona Gage (Morella), David Frankham (Dr Eliot James).

Crew: Director/Producer Roger Corman, Writer Richard Matheson, Cinematography Floyd Crosby, Music Les Baxter, Editor Anthony Carras, Art Director Daniel Haller, Special Effects Pat Dinga, 120/90 minutes.

Story: Morella: Returning home after being abandoned 26 years before, Lenora is shocked to find it a decaying pile, her father, Locke, a drunken recluse, and her dead mother, Morella, a mummified corpse in the bedroom. Lenora tells Locke that she is dying; Locke that Morella blamed Lenora for her own death. That night, Morella revives and possesses Lenora's body. She strangles Locke and the house collapses in a blazing ruin. Morella returns to her own body, triumphant.

The Black Cat: Alcoholic Montresor forever bullies Annabel, his wife, for money and detests her cat. One evening he bests Fortunato, a dapper connoisseur, at a wine-tasting. Fortunato carries him home and immediately falls for Annabel. Suddenly, Montresor is given all the drinking money he needs. But when he discovers the affair, he kills Annabel. Subduing Fortunato with a drugged Amontillado, Montresor walls them both up in the cellar. In his cups that night, Montresor arouses the barman's suspicions. The next morning, the police awake Montresor. Despite the DTs, he shows them around. In the cellar, he perversely raps on the wall. An ungodly wail arises. Tearing down the wall, the police find the bodies and Annabel's cat, which Monstresor has unwittingly interred alive.

The Case Of M Valdemar: Valdemar is dying. To ease his pain, he allows Carmichael to hypnotise him. The treatment works. However, both Valdemar's wife, Helene, and his physician, James, distrust the hypnotist. Valdemar allays their fears and begs Helene to marry James after he dies. Carmichael has other ideas. He hypnotises Valdemar at the point of death and refuses release until Valdemar orders Helene to marry him. When Helene agrees on the condition Carmichael frees Valdemar, Carmichael attacks her. Stirred by her cries, Valdemar's decaying body rises and throttles Carmichael.

Background: After the (lesser) success of *The Premature Burial*, Corman changed tack with this portmanteau offering. Adapting three stories for *Tales Of Terror* instead of one meant that screenwriter Matheson needed to add little in the way of padding or extra sub-plots to Poe's original tales. Although billed as three stories, *The Black Cat* segment amalgamates elements of *The Black Cat* with *The Cask Of Amontillado*, thus rather neatly avoiding the graphic animal cruelty of the former.

Given another fifteen-day shoot, each story was filmed in a week. It took over $1.5 million in rentals and encouraged Corman to continue his relationship with Poe and Matheson a little longer. *The Premature Burial* had added a small amount of sly humour to the horror and Matheson had done a similar trick for *The Black Cat*. Here the humour was more overt and Lorre and Price worked well with each other, despite their different acting backgrounds. The film's approach and success would convince Corman that there was still some mileage left in adapting Poe.

Verdict: At first sight, *Tales Of Terror* appears an odd mixture. *Morella* teeters on the brink of parody and the climax of *Valdemar* feels hurried but there are *moments*. And these moments ultimately make up for any faults in the execution. The finest being where *The Black Cat* suddenly segues from knockabout humour into chilling dialogue quoted exactly from *The Cask Of Amontillado*: 'For the love of God, Montresor!' pleads Price, finally aware of his fate. 'Yes,' replies Lorre, casually sliding another brick into place, 'For the love of God.'3/5

Tower Of London (1962)

Cast: Vincent Price (Richard of Gloucester), Michael Pate (Sir Ratcliffe), Joan Freeman (Lady Margaret), Robert Brown (Sir Justin), Justice Watson (Edward IV), Sara Selby (Queen Elizabeth), Richard McCauly (Clarence), Eugene Martin (Prince Edward), Donald Losby (Prince Richard), Sandra Knight (Mistress Shore), Richard Hale (Tyrus), Bruce Gordon (Earl of Buckingham), Joan Camden (Anne).

Crew: Director Roger Corman, Producer Gene Corman, Writers Leo V Gordon, F Amos Powell, James B Gordon, Cinematography Arch R Dalzell, Music Michael Anderson, Editor Ronald Sinclair, 79 minutes.

Story: 1483. England is in the grip of war and King Edward IV is on his deathbed. His brother Richard, goaded by Anne, his wife, plans to succeed the throne, but must destroy those in his way. These include his other brother, the Duke of Clarence, the young princes, Richard and Edward, and those faithful to Edward IV's widow, Elizabeth and the house of Woodville. With each murder, Richard's victims return to haunt him, prophesying that he will die at Bosworth (a place he has never heard of) by the hand of a dead man. One ghost even drives him to strangle Anne, further isolating him. But, despite the best efforts of the Woodville faithful, Richard murders the young princes in the tower and is crowned King of England. However, armies loyal to Elizabeth rise against him and his army is defeated at Bosworth. Richard, believing his army still lives, is confronted by the ghosts of his victims and falls to his death on the blade of a battleaxe held by one of his dead soldiers.

Background: Not so much a travesty of history as the standard biased Tudor view of Richard III recycled for a drive-in audience. Edward Small, head of Admiral Pictures, was looking for a way to cash in on the success of Corman's Poe movies and Corman was looking for a break from Poe, so between them they arrived at *Tower Of London*. Not to be confused with Rowland V Lee's superior 1939 version, which starred Boris Karloff as executioner Mord, Basil Rathbone as Richard and Price as Clarence. Corman's version strikes no balance between elective (Richard) and predestined (Mord) villainies. By removing Mord's character in this version, Richard takes all the responsibility and goes mad in the process.

Verdict: Despite his excellence in the Poe movies, Price's performance in *Tower* becomes increasingly hammy towards the final battle. The low budget is on display in scenes such as the cut-price Battle of Bosworth Field and, despite some atmospheric moments, the cumulative effect is one of a cheap pageant of horrors rather than a truly horrific film about the corruptive nature of ambition. 3/5

The Young Racers (1963)

Cast: Mark Damon (Stephen Children), William Campbell (Joe Machin), Luana Anders (Henny), Robert Campbell (Robert Machin), Marie Versini (Sesia Machin), Patrick Magee (Sir William Dragonet), Christine Gregg (Daphne), John McLaren (Lotus Team Manager), Beatrice Altariba (Monique), Margreta Robsahn (Lea), Milo Quesada (Italian driver), Anthony Marsh (Announcer).

Crew: Producer/Director Roger Corman, Writer R Wright Campbell, Cinematography Floyd Crosby, Music Les Baxter, Editor Ronald Sinclair, Art Director Albert Locatelli, Technical Advisor Anthony Marsh, 82 minutes.

Story: Joe Machin wins the Monte Carlo Grand Prix but only by endangering other drivers. His private life is equally reckless. He pursues a very public affair with Monique, fiancée of ex-racer Stephen Children. Now a successful novelist, Stephen catches the couple smooching at a café and plans to expose Joe's philandering in his next book. Stephen gets Joe's consent to follow him through the races, and Lotus team's permission to drive with them. Although driven by revenge, Stephen begins to admire Joe. In England, Sir William Dragonet, previously cuckolded by Joe relishes telling him of Monique and Stephen's relationship, and Stephen's plan. During the race at Aintree, Joe and Stephen both try to kill each other but Joe has a change of heart. Swerving to avoid hitting Stephen's car, he crashes.

Months later, Stephen visits Joe and gives him a copy of the toned-down book. He is greeted warmly, the accident having made Joe reject his old lifestyle and settle down with his wife.

Background: Corman planned to shoot around the Grand Prix races in the same way that he had completed his previous projects in Hawaii and Puerto Rico: get his crew to come along on token salaries and pay for their travelling costs, giving them a sort of holiday in the process. AIP gave him a budget of $150,000 and he saved extensive equipment and transportation costs by using a converted Volkswagen microbus as a mobile studio. With no work permits, he relied mainly on the organisation of his PA, Mary Anne Wood, and the goodwill of the Lotus and Cooper Formula 1 teams, including their top drivers at the time, Jimmy Clark and Bill McClaren. Machin wore a Team Lotus helmet for the close-ups and then Corman would film Clark racing and cut the shots together. For Machin's personal car, Corman secured the use of a Sunbeam by giving it on-screen promotion. It was the only car to crash during the film's production. Driving it from Monte Carlo to Paris for the next race, Charles Griffith and his girlfriend were pushed off the road by a skidding camper van. They survived, the Sunbeam didn't. Machin had to walk into shot from then on.

For the script he hired R Wright Campbell to rewrite a bullfighting love-triangle story that he had been trying to sell to Fox. Campbell also played Machin's brother (no big challenge as it really was his brother, William). He's not great, but he did have Bell's Palsy at the time. Assistant directing duties went to Robert Towne, Charles Griffith and a USC film school student called Menachem Golan who, for better or worse, would become president of Cannon Films (home of *Lemon Popsicle*, Michael Winner and Chuck Norris). Also along, as soundman, grip and first assistant was Francis Ford Coppola.

Verdict: Practically shot on the run, *Racers* manages to convey both the excitement of Grand Prix racing and low-budget film-making. While the plot is nothing new, everyone gets into the fun of it (a paid European vacation can't have hurt) and Corman is clearly enjoying himself among a crew of old friends that he refers to in his biography as 'one of the all-time great(s)'. 4/5

The Raven (1963)

Cast: Vincent Price (Dr Erasmus Craven), Peter Lorre (Dr Bedlo), Boris Karloff (Dr Scarabus), Hazel Court (Lenore Craven), Jack Nicholson (Rexford Bedlo), Olive Sturgess (Estelle Craven).

Crew: Director/Producer Roger Corman, Writer Richard Matheson, Cinematography Floyd Crosby, Music Les Baxter, Editor Ronald Sinclair, Art Director Daniel Haller, Special Effects Pat Dinga, 86 minutes.

Story: Reclusive Erasmus Craven still mourns the death of his wife, Lenore. One night, he's visited by a talking raven. It's Dr Bedlo, transformed by the powerful sorcerer, Dr Scarabus, after challenging him to a duel. Craven remembers Scarabus as his late father's rival for head of the magician's guild. Craven has inherited his father's ability for hand-gesture magic, which Scarabus covets. Craven changes Bedlo back. He informs Craven that Scarabus is holding Lenore's spirit prisoner. And so, along with Craven's daughter, Estelle, and Bedlo's dozy son, Rexford, the two sorcerers set off for Scarabus' castle. Bedlo, however, is working for Scarabus. Scarabus is welcoming at first, but then kills Bedlo and imprisons the others. Craven finds Lenore faked her death in order to live with Scarabus. Bedlo, it transpires, did the same to continue his duplicity and help the others escape. Caught by Scarabus, Bedlo is turned back into a raven. Scarabus tortures Estelle so Craven will yield up his magic secrets. While raven-Bedlo frees the others, a magical duel ensues between Scarabus and Craven. The castle collapses around the still-bickering Scarabus and Lenore, and the triumphant Craven leads the others home. However, he decides not to re-transmogrify Bedlo.

Background: Aware that the Poe movies were in danger of becoming stale and losing their audience, Corman decided to build on *The Black Cat* and combine humour and horror throughout the movie. Richard Matheson was again hired to write the script (which, aside from a couple of nice gags at its expense, has nothing to do with Poe's most famous poem) and Daniel Haller again built upon the sets gained from the previous movies, giving Scarabus' castle a much grander look. When first confronted with the script, Price, Lorre and Karloff, aware that it was supposed to be a comedy, were concerned by how straight it seemed, so they wrote many of the broader laughs themselves. All changes were approved by Corman who, according to Karloff, was more concerned that his camera set-ups and lighting were to his satisfaction. '"You're experienced actors, get on with it," he told us.'

There were problems however. Karloff was a classically trained actor and stuck rigidly to the script. Lorre had a more improvisational spirit, and was continually adding extra bits to the material as he went along. Price, who'd already worked with Lorre in *The Black Cat* segment of *Tales Of*

Terror, was used to this approach and even added material himself. Nicholson happily threw in his lot with Lorre. Scenes where Nicholson continually fusses with Lorre's cloak were improvised to gain a reaction, annoying Lorre and making their on-screen relationship ('He takes after his mother' confides Bedlo, sourly) more convincing. Karloff, however, wasn't pleased, the improvisation continually throwing him off his performance. In the end, Price acted as a go-between, putting Karloff at ease by playing their scenes as written whilst improvising when on screen with Lorre. The scenes between Lorre and Karloff were tolerated, but not enjoyed. The other problem, as Jack Nicholson recalls, was the raven: 'It used to shit over everybody and everything,' he comments in Corman's autobiography. 'It just shit endlessly. My whole right shoulder was constantly covered with raven shit.'

Verdict: Fortunately, *The Raven* is a model of sardonic good humour, with Corman's lightness of touch giving everyone room to shine. Haller's sets are particularly impressive, here getting their final airing before Corman took his Poe adaptations to England, with Scarabus' castle a triumph of the 'hoarding ethic'. 5/5

The Terror (1963)

aka *The Castle Of Terror*, *Lady Of The Shadows*

Cast: Boris Karloff (Baron Von Leppe), Jack Nicholson (André Duvalier), Sandra Knight (Helene), Richard Miller (Stefan), Dorothy Neumann (Witch Woman), Jonathan Haze (Gustaf).

Crew: Producer/Director Roger Corman, Location Director Jack Hill, Writers Leo Gordon, Jack Hill, Cinematography John Nicolaus, Music Ronald Stein, Editor Stuart O'Brien, Art Director Daniel Haller, 81 minutes.

Story: Separated from his regiment, Napoleonic soldier Duvalier meets Helene, a strange young woman who gives him water and disappears. Rescued by Gustaf, a witch's servant, Duvalier is told that Helene is the witch's eagle. Duvalier is sceptical. Meeting Helene again, she leads him into quicksand. Saving Duvalier again, Gustaf tells him Helene is possessed and can only be helped if Duvalier goes to Baron Von Leppe's castle. At the castle, Duvalier sees Helene, who ignores him, but is welcomed by Von Leppe and his manservant, Stefan. Von Leppe has been a recluse for twenty years, ever since he killed his wife, Isle, for cuckolding him with local boy Eric. Stefan killed Eric. Later, Stefan visits Eric's house and sees the witch hypnotising Helene into believing she is Ilse. Duvalier leaves but is sent back to the castle to save Helene by Gustaf, who is killed by the witch's eagle. Meanwhile, at Ilse's spectral bidding, Von Leppe prepares to flood the crypt and drown, unaware that the witch, Eric's mother, has planned this. Rather than reunite him with Ilse, his suicide will send him to Hell. Duvalier, the witch and Stefan reach the castle. Stefan reveals that, actually, Eric killed the baron and took his place. The witch is killed by lightning, and Eric floods the crypt. Only Duvalier and Helene survive the deluge. As they kiss, Helene rots away.

Background: Famously, *The Terror* was made because Karloff still owed AIP three days work after *The Raven* was completed. Or because *The Raven* sets were about to be torn down and Corman wanted to get another movie out of them before they disappeared, this time for his own company, Film-group. Either way, Karloff's scenes were filmed over a weekend. *The Raven* finished shooting on a Friday, Corman got the crew to leave striking the sets until Monday and rang up Leo Gordon. With the scenes Gordon wrote, Corman filmed over the weekend with Karloff, Nicholson and Dick Miller. While the sets were being pulled down, Corman was still racing around with Karloff and the cameraman. Three months later, Corman called Miller to tell him that they were going to finish the movie. Miller by this point had gained twenty pounds in weight. It wasn't even Corman who finished shooting it, but several other would-be directors including Jack Hill, Monte Hellman, Francis Ford Coppola and Jack Nicholson, over a period of months.

Verdict: For a film as legendarily plotless as *The Terror* there is an awful lot going on, unfortunately not a great deal of it makes much sense. Everyone involved inserted their own twopenn'orth. So much so that Nicholson's pitch for directing to Corman was simply 'Everyone in this whole damned town's directed this picture. Let me direct the last day.' Realising that it couldn't make much difference, Corman accepted. 3/5

X (1963)

aka *X - The Man With X-Ray Eyes*

Cast: Ray Milland (Dr James Xavier), Diana Van Der Vlis (Dr Diane Fairfax), Harold J Stone (Dr Sam Brant), John Hoyt (Dr Willard Benson), Don Rickles (Crane), John Dierkes (Preacher), Lorrie Summers (Party Dancer), Vicki Lee (Young Girl Patient), Kathryn Hart (Mrs Mart), Dick Miller, Jonathan Haze (Hecklers).

Crew: Producer/Director Roger Corman, Writers Robert Dillon, Ray Russell, Cinematography Floyd Crosby, Music Les Baxter, Editor Anthony Carras, Art Director Daniel Haller, Special Effects Butler-Glouner Inc. 80 Minutes.

Story: Dr James Xavier creates a serum to increase the field of human vision. When his funding is threatened due to lack of results, he tries it on himself. Both his colleague, Dr Brant and funding representative, Diane Fairfax, express misgivings. Administered as eyedrops, chemical 'X' gives

Xavier x-ray vision but shocks him unconscious. Unable to defend his experiments, his funding is withdrawn. However, Xavier continues to administer the drops, increasing the power of his vision but necessitating thick goggles. Suspended on a trumped-up malpractice charge, Xavier accidentally kills Brant and goes on the run. He surfaces as a carnival mind-reading act, managed by the venal Crane. Believing Xavier has healing powers, Crane exploits him for financial gain. Rescued by Diane, they drive to Las Vegas where Xavier uses his power to bilk the casinos for anti-serum funding. His plan collapses when his goggles are removed. Pursued by the police he flees to the desert where he stumbles into a revival meeting. There, Xavier tells the congregation what horrors he now sees waiting outside the universe. When the preacher preaches 'If thine eye offend thee, pluck it out,' Xavier does so.

Background: It is rumoured that the original climax to the movie went one stage further. After plucking out his eyes, Xavier supposedly exclaimed: 'I can still see!' Corman chose instead to freeze on Xavier's empty sockets, allegedly because the line was too frightening. *X*, as with many AIP movies, started life as a title thought up by James Nicholson. Various characters were considered, including a jazz musician and a burglar, before Xavier as a medical researcher came into being. Shot on a three-week schedule with a budget somewhere between $200,000 and $300,000, Milland took a sizeable cut which left little for the special effects. While the pre-psychedelia 'Spectarama' optical effects look fairly cheapjack, they do manage to convey much of Xavier's disorientating situation. Corman bolstered this with trick photography such as filming a building in progress when only steel girders were showing and then returning to the site three months later and filming the completed building. By reversing these shots, Xavier 'saw' through the building. Elsewhere in the film, to ensure a wide cinema distribution, the party scene, where Xavier sees through the dancers clothing, treats audiences to a display of bare shins, ankles and shoulders.

Verdict: Whilst never a truly great film, *X* forms a bridge between the mad doctor movies of the Thirties and Forties and the more evolutionary 'body-horror' of David Cronenberg from the Seventies onwards. Xavier's journey from visionary to voyeur to fake seer to real seer is aided by Milland's gravitas. Haller's grey and brown sets add a realistic counterpoint to Xavier's dazzling visions. Crosby's camerawork once again proves vital to Corman's personal vision, most notably in the 180° tracking shot around Xavier as the first drops are administered, ending with the back of his head and then fading into our view of his optic nerves as he 'sees' for the first time. 4/5

The Haunted Palace (1963)

Cast: Vincent Price (Charles Dexter Ward/Joseph Curwen), Debra Paget (Ann Ward), Lon Chaney Jr. (Simon Orne), Frank Maxwell (Dr Marinus Willet), Leo Gordon (Edgar Weedon), Elisha Cook Jr. (Peter Smith), John Dierkes (Jacob West), Harry Ellerbe (Minister), Cathy Merchant (Hester Tillinghast), Milton Parsons (Jabez Hutchinson), Guy Wilkerson (Leach), Darlene Lucht (Young Victim), Barboura Morris (Mrs Weeden), Bruno Ve Sota (Bartender).

Crew: Director/Producer Roger Corman, Writer Charles Beaumont, Cinematography Floyd Crosby, Music Ronald Stein, Editor Ronald Sinclair, Art Director Daniel Haller, 85 minutes.

Story: 18th Century Arkham, New England. After sacrificing women to the Old Ones (an evil race banished from earth eons before mankind) warlock Joseph Curwen is burned alive by the villagers, but not before he has cursed his persecutors and their descendents. 110 years later, Curwen's great-great-grandson, Charles Dexter Ward, and his wife, Ann, arrive in Arkham to claim their inheritance. They get a chilly reception from the locals and are shocked by their mutated offspring. Willett, the local doctor, directs them to Curwen's palace. There, Charles notices his resemblance to his ancestor's portrait and through it Curwen starts to possess him. The Wards meet the caretaker, Simon, actually one of Curwen's fellow warlocks there to oversee the possession. As Curwen's power grows, Charles becomes increasingly brutal towards Ann. He starts killing off his persecutors' descendents and reconnects with the Old Ones. These activities stir up the locals anew. Ann is captured by the warlocks for sacrifice to Curwen's gods. Willet rescues her as the mob torch the palace. As Curwen's portrait burns, his power over Charles fades, allowing him to escape the blazing ruin. But Curwen might still triumph…

Background: Eager not to do another Poe movie, Corman suggested an adaptation of HP Lovecraft's novella *The Case Of Charles Dexter Ward*, one of the lengthier entries in his Cthulhu Mythos series. In fact, he had been planning it since *The Premature Burial* and intended it to star Boris Karloff, Ray Milland and Hazel Court. The film was to be entitled *The Haunted Village*. However, Nicholson and Arkoff, equally keen not to buck the success of the cycle, insisted that the title was changed to *The Haunted Palace*, thus tying in with the poem that Poe included as part of *The Fall Of The House Of Usher*. Price and Debra Paget were thus cast and, with Karloff unwell, Lon Chaney Jr. stepped into the role of Simon. Corman relented and Vincent Price can be heard reading two verses from the poem during the film, but the plot, for anyone who has read Lovecraft, is quite clearly set in his world. The combination might well have pleased Lovecraft himself, who worshipped Poe from an early age, and set out to 'unlearn' as many modern words as possible in order to sound more like his literary god.

This was also the first film in which Corman experimented with a then recent innovation: the zoom lens. In an interview in 1984, he recalled: 'They were much slower than the normal fixed lens, and as a result you had to pour light on the set in order to reach an intensity that a zoom lens could photograph.' His use of this piece of equipment is particularly striking in the scene when Ward bids Dr Willett to take Ann back to Boston. As they leave, there is a zoom in on Ward's face, which ends by framing his head in the frame of Curwen's portrait.

Verdict: Anyone attempting to review *The Haunted Palace* from its source material is on a hiding to nowhere. It has nothing to do with Poe (whose name is misspelt in the opening credits) and Lovecraft's atmospherics, as always, remain too elusive to adapt properly. Daniel Haller's sets, the musty greys and greens forever threatening to envelope the characters, while impressive as ever, are Poe by default. Lovecraft's Cthulhu Mythos dealt with the repossession of Earth by its evil previous inhabitants. Only in the film's climactic scenes does this theme begin to emerge and by then the rhubarbing locals are storming the set with their torches. 3/5

The Secret Invasion (1964)

Cast: Stewart Granger (Major Richard Mace), Raf Vallone (Roberto Rocca), Henry Silva (John Durrell), Mickey Rooney (Terrence Scanlon), Edd Byrnes (Simon Fell), William Campbell (Jean Saval), Mia Massini (Mila), Helmo Kindermann (German Fortress Commandant), Enzo Fiermonte (General Quadri).

Crew: Producer/Director Roger Corman, Writer R Wright Campbell, Cinematography Arthur E Arling, Music Hugo Freidhofer, Editor Ronald Sinclair, Special Effects George Blackwell, 95 minutes.

Story: During World War II, five convicts are chosen by British intelligence to rescue the Italian General Quadri from a Dubrovnik prison in return for their freedom. The five, conveniently including a demolitions expert, a master criminal, a forger and an assassin, are headed by Major Mace. They use their talents to reach the prison, but are captured by the Nazis before they can free Quadri. Inside the jail, they realise that Quadri is an impostor who has killed the original. Despite fatalities, the group escape from the jail disguised as Nazis and force 'Quadri' to address his troops and convince them that the Germans are their enemies. He is then killed before he can renounce his speech. Thus the Italians turn on the Nazis and the war is won, but at what cost?

Background: One of Corman's worst directing experiences. Corman was approached by David Picker, head of production at United Artists, some time before to do a project but had never come up with anything UA approved. However R Wright Campbell had written a script, originally titled 'The Dubious Patriots' (a reworking of *Five Guns West*) which Picker liked. Gene Corman had negotiated the shoot with United Artists at a budget of $600,000, to be filmed on location in Yugoslavia. Originally, UA had planned to send an auditor to keep an eye on finances but, since the auditor's wage would come out of the budget, Gene talked UA out of it, leaving the budget clear for the film.

Corman soon realised that the six-week shoot to produce a 'big-looking' film was going to be beyond his abilities. Almost. For a start, he never got the military equipment and troops that he was promised; they had been redirected to help with an emergency earthquake relief. Rolf, his Yugoslavian production assistant, turned out not to be that well adjusted. He cleared a beach set for a scene by pulling his gun on holidaymakers. Then there was *Invasion*'s lead, Stewart Granger. Granger was a now-fading matinee idol who had found fame with Gainsborough Pictures during the Forties. He was well aware that appearing in an independent picture was a comedown for him, but when he realised how small the budget was, it had a big impact. Granger thus proved extremely difficult to work with. Matters came to a head during a night scene. Granger refused to work until he could use a key line that had been written for Edd Byrnes's character. Byrnes was perfectly happy to continue without Granger but the scene wouldn't have worked like that. After nearly an hour's deadlock, Corman came up with a line for Granger that was an equivalent of Byrnes' line, allowing them, and filming, to go ahead. Undaunted by the experience, Corman brought in *Invasion* for around $592,000 and on time, to boot. It grossed over £3 million.

However, there is a punchline. In his first experience of working for a big studio (albeit UA), Corman received a distribution report that stated that they were still $200,000 short of breaking even. Obviously Corman queried this and suggested an audit. UA offered to buy his participation out for $400,000 so long as he didn't audit. Ever the businessman, Corman took the money and signed away his rights, attesting that UA's bookkeeping was 'true and accurate'. With his honeymoon with the majors well and truly over, Corman returned to AIP for another crack at Poe.

Verdict: 2/5

The Masque Of The Red Death (1964)

Cast: Vincent Price (Prince Prospero), Hazel Court (Juliana), Jane Asher (Francesca), David Weston (Gino), Patrick Magee (Alfredo), Nigel Green (Ludovico), Skip Martin (Hop Toad), John Westbrook (Man in Red), Julian Burton (Senor Veronese), Doreen Dawn (Anna-Marie), Paul Whitsun-Jones (Scarlatti), Jean Lodge (Scarlatti's Wife), Verina Greenlaw (Esmeralda).

Crew: Producer/Director Roger Corman, Writers Charles Beaumont, R Wright Campbell, Cinematography Nicolas Roeg, Music David Lee, Editor Ann Chegwidden, Production Design Daniel Haller, Art Direction Robert Jones, Special Effects George Blackwell, 90/86/84 minutes.

Story: The Middle Ages. With the Red Death sweeping Europe, Prince Prospero and his guests seal themselves within his castle, certain they'll be safe from the plague. From the local village that he's ordered to be destroyed, Prospero brings Francesca, an innocent peasant girl, her lover Gino and her father, Ludovico. Revels are planned, including a great masked ball. Prospero encourages his guests to debase themselves for his amusement and he instructs Francesca, a devout Christian, in the ways of his own master, Satan. Prospero's lover, Juliana, gives her soul to Satan and tries to aid the three captives' escape, but their plan is discovered, Juliana is destroyed by Satan, Ludovico is killed trying to kill Prospero and Gino is forced from the castle to die of the plague. As the masquerade gets under way, Prospero's sadistic friend, Alfredo, is lured into a fiery death by Hop Toad, a dwarf whose love, Esmeralda, Alfredo struck. Prospero spies a person cowled in red, a colour forbidden to his guests. Believing him to be Satan, Prospero pursues him. Confronting the guest, Prospero negotiates Francesca's freedom, having recognised in her a faith as great as his own. She is spared, but not by Satan. The visitor is the Red Death and Prospero and his guests perish, leaving only Gino and Francesca alive in the wake of the plague.

Background: Corman returned to Britain for *Masque* after Arkoff struck a co-production deal with AIP's UK distributors, Anglo-Amalgamated. While he felt rather alienated working with a British crew, his choices were faultless, not least in using cinematographer Nicolas Roeg who would later direct that other great red-obsessed horror film *Don't Look Now*. For the sets, Corman and Haller had access to the scene docks at Elstree. Using sets from historical epics such as *Becket* and *A Man For All Seasons* gave *Masque* a size and grandeur that their previous Poe collaborations had never quite reached. The original screenplay by Charles Beaumont didn't achieve what he wanted, so Corman brought in R Wright Campbell and got him to rework Beaumont's screenplay adding Poe's *Hop-Frog* into the tale.

Verdict: Corman's most coherent Poe adaptation since *Usher.* The colours of the film, particularly in the coded sequence of the chambers through which Prospero and Francesca pursue the red figure, are stunning. Roeg's restless camera, prowling the halls and performing dizzying 360° turns during Price's speech about the anatomy of fear and at the climactic *danse macabre*, adds further layers of unease to a film never satisfied with being a straightforward horror movie. Price's impressive performance as Prospero (only bettered by his cynical religious maniac in *Witchfinder General*), presents a man whose 'evil' is never black and white but more a reaction to the god-forsaken times in which he lives. Even he is disgusted by the venality and brutishness of those at his court. *Masque* remains Corman's most complex horror film, and one of the genre's definitive movies. 5/5

The Tomb Of Ligeia (1965)

aka *Ligeia, Last Tomb Of Ligeia, Tomb Of The Cat*

Cast: Vincent Price (Verden Fell), Elizabeth Shepherd (Rowena/Ligeia), John Westbrook (Christopher Gough), Oliver Johnston (Kenrick), Derek Francis (Lord Trevanion), Richard Vernon (Dr Vivian), Ronald Adam (Parson), Frank Thornton (Peperel), Denis Gilmore (Livery Boy).

Crew: Producer/Director Roger Corman, Co-Producer Pat Green, Writer Robert Towne, Cinematography Arthur Grant, Music Kenneth V Jones, Editor Alfred Cox, Art Director Colin Couthcott, Special Effects Ted Samuels, 81 minutes.

Story: England, 1872. Verden Fell inters his late wife Ligeia within the ruins of the abbey where they lived. During the burial, a black cat suddenly appears and Ligeia opens her eyes. Although Fell tells himself it was a contraction of her nerves, Ligeia's previous claims that her will could conquer death makes him a recluse. Months later, a fox-hunt brings Rowena to his door, after her horse throws her at Ligeia's tomb. An uneasy first encounter blossoms into love and Fell and Rowena soon marry. During their honeymoon, Fell is a changed man but he relapses on their return. Hired to sell the abbey, Fell's lawyer, Gough, tells him that the abbey was in Ligeia's name and there is no death certificate. Fell withdraws from Rowena, disappearing at night when she needs him most. Her nightmares, and an experiment in mesmerism, increasingly blur her personality with Ligeia's. One night, Gough exhumes Ligeia to find a wax effigy and Rowena discovers a secret chamber where Fell keeps Ligeia's body. Realising Ligeia mesmerized Fell before her death to believe she still lived, Rowena tries to awaken him from his trance but loses consciousness after cutting herself on a broken mirror. Fell burns Ligeia's body, igniting the abbey. He then throttles Rowena before pursuing the cat, seeing Ligeia's spirit in them both. As the abbey burns, Gough rescues Rowena but Fell perishes, seemingly alongside Ligeia.

Background: Yes, it is complicated, isn't it? Towne's script confused Corman so much he had to keep a chart showing where Ligeia's spirit was supposed to be at any given time. Filmed on location in a crumbling abbey in Norfolk, the settings (interiors filmed at Shepperton) however are a vast change from studio-bound adaptations. Here, Poe's atmosphere of death and obsession can be seen to affect the 'real' world and the location work by Hammer Film's Arthur Grant allows for daylight to be cast over the shadows. This plays a vital part in a story that relies very much on vision, particularly Fell's vision. Towne's screenplay teases out threads from Poe's extremely short story to create a meditation on the dead's survival through those who grieve for them. Ultimately, *Ligeia* faces fears that we all must face at some time in our lives: How do we let those we love (whether living or dead) go without our own personality being destroyed in the process?

Verdict: Corman allows free rein to his Freudian impulses and fills the film with heavily symbolic images – the black cat, the journey up the bell tower, the secret room behind a mirror that reflects not Rowena, but Ligeia. Shepherd in the dual roles of Fell's living and dead loves further deepens the film's complexity. Less sensational than *Masque*, *Ligeia* only falters because of Towne's confusion and the near Corman/Poe parody of its climax. 4/5

5: Outside Looking In (1966-70)

'I did some hanging out at parties with the Angels. Their beer parties were just like anyone else's, except they listened to the Stones doing "Satisfaction" about a hundred and fifty times in a row'

Peter Fonda

During the filming of *Ligeia,* Corman was approached by Columbia Pictures. Seeing this as an opportunity to graduate to bigger films and to escape making further Poe films, Corman signed up. It was a fraught relationship. Columbia only wanted Corman for his abilities to turn in low-budget, short schedule pictures. After Columbia scuppered both his adaptation of Kafka's *In The Penal Colony* and a film about Iwo Jima, they finally gave him the go-ahead for a Robert Towne-scripted Western *The Long Ride Home.* Corman directed a few scenes before further disagreements led to him walking off the project and, by mutual consent, out of his contract. Eager to direct again after such a creatively frustrating time, Corman returned to AIP.

The Wild Angels (1966)

Cast: Peter Fonda (Heavenly Blues), Nancy Sinatra (Mike), Bruce Dern (Loser), Lou Procopio (Joint), Coby Denton (Bull Puckey), Marc Cavell (Frankenstein), Buck Taylor (Dear John), Norm Alden (Medic), Michael J Pollard (Pigmy), Diane Ladd (Gaysh), Joan Shawlee (Momma Monahan), Gayle Hunnicut (Suzie), Art Baker (Thomas), Frank Maxwell (Preacher), Frank Gerstle (Hospital Policeman), Kim Hamilton (Nurse), Peter Bogdanovich and members of the Hell's Angels, Venice, California.

Crew: Director/Producer Roger Corman, Writer Charles B Griffith, Cinematography Richard Moore, Music Mike Curb, Editor Monte Hellman, Art Director Leon Ericksen, 90 minutes.

Story: Blues, the president of a Californian branch of the Hell's Angels, tracks down a stolen chopper belonging to his best friend, Loser. Gathering together the rest of the gang, they drive down to Mecca, a small desert town where the bike has been taken to a chop shop. Their rumble with the Mexicans who run the place alerts the Highway Patrol who give chase. Loser steals one of their bikes and is shot, a Highway patrolman crashes and dies. After being operated on, Loser is held in hospital, pending transfer to jail. With the aid of Blues' old lady, Mike, the Angels spring him but it's a bad idea and he dies soon afterwards. Gathering for his funeral, Blues has a showdown with the preacher and the service degenerates into a drunken party-cum-fight. They take the coffin for burial but the local townspeople attack them. In the ensuing fight, only Blues, disillusioned by the whole situation, stays behind to bury Loser and face the police.

Background: Inspired by a photograph on the cover of *Life* magazine of Hell's Angels on their way to a member's funeral, Corman took the idea to AIP. Almost immediately there was conflict over what direction the story should take. Nicholson and Arkoff wanted a reworking of the town-terrorised-by-bikers angle from *The Wild One* (1954); Corman insisted that the film should be told from the Angels' viewpoint. AIP relented and gave him a budget of $360,000. *Angels* turned out to be AIP's most financially successful film, swiftly taking over $5 million in rentals.

Corman and Griffith did research by hanging out with Hell's Angels in East and South Central LA; by keeping the bikers in pot and booze they got to hear enough stories for Griffith to hammer out a screenplay. Corman struck many of his casting deals at the same time, offering to pay each Angel $35 a day with an extra $20 for their bike, and $15 if they brought their 'old lady'. Before filming, the script was overhauled considerably by an uncredited Peter Bogdanovich, then a film reviewer for *Esquire* magazine. Casting had to be overhauled. First choice for Blues (originally named Jack Black) was George Chakiris who had come to fame in *West Side Story*. Chakiris, however, was reluctant to ride a motorcycle. He begged Corman for a stunt double after one lesson. Aiming for realism, rather than doubles and cutaways, Corman refused. Chakiris dropped out and Fonda and Dern were bumped up the cast list.

Shooting, around Venice, San Pedro and the desert and mountains around Palm Springs, was difficult. Many of the Angels resented Corman's authority so collected their money and then drifted away. Corman tried his best to strike a balance between being The Man and a doormat, but this edginess comes across on the screen. He managed to hold the Angels' interest by plying them with beer and grass. The Angels' bikes didn't always work to order; being old and in poor repair they often took ages to get started, especially in the cold mountain air. Plus, the entire shoot was under constant surveillance from the local police and, it's rumoured, the CIA, keen to bust many of the Angels on outstanding warrants.

Verdict: In spite of, or perhaps because of, these problems, *Angels* emerges as a raw, objective movie, enhanced by Corman's let's-just-get-this-finished approach, Hellman's tight editing and some impressive hand-held camera work. With the lessons that Corman learned from *The Intruder*, *Angels* compensates for its near-documentary approach with lashings of exploitation-friendly sex, drugs and violence. Arguably, it is his definitive meditation on 'the outsider'; with the definitive outsiders as his subject-matter, it's not hard to see why. 5/5

The St Valentine's Day Massacre (1967)

Cast: Jason Robards Jr. (Al Capone), George Segal (Peter Gusenberg), Ralph Meeker (George 'Bugs' Moran), Jean Hale (Myrtle Nelson), Clint Ritchie (Machine Gun Jack McGurn), Frank Silvera (Nicholas Sorello), Joseph Campanella (Al Wienshank), Richard Bakalyan (John Scalisi), David Canary (Frank Gusenberg), Bruce Dern (Johnny May), Harold J Stone (Frank Nitti), Kurt Krueger (James Clark), Paul Richards (Charles Fischetti), Joseph Turkel (Jack Guzik), Milton Frome (Adam Heyer), Mickey Deems (Reinhart Schwimmer), John Agar (Dion O'Bannon), Celia Lovsky (Josephine Schwimmer), Tom Reese (Ted Newberry), Jan Merlin (Willie Marks), Alex D'Arcy (Kymie Weiss), Gus Trikonis (Rio), Charles Dierkop (Salvanti), Tom Signorelli (Bobo Borotto), Rico Cattani (Albert Anselmi), Alex D'Arcy (Joe Aiello), Alex Rocco (Diamond), Leo Gordon (James Morton), Barboura Morris (Jeanette Landsman), Mary Grace Canfield (Mrs Doody), Ron Gans (Chapman), Jack Del Rio, Phil Haran, Nob Brandin, Ernesto Moralli, Nick Morgani (Capone's Board Members), Ken Scott (Policeman), Joan Shawlee (Edna), Jack Nicholson (Gino), Paul Frees (Narrator), Dick Miller, Jonathan Haze (Uncredited Mobsters).

Crew: Producer/Director Roger Corman, Writer Howard Browne, Cinematography Milton Krasner, Music Fred Steiner, Editor William B Murphy, Art Directors Jack Martin Smith, Philip Jefferies, 100 minutes.

Story: Chicago, the late Twenties. Prohibition has enabled mobsters to rise to power, setting up over 12,000 speakeasies in that city alone. The dominant groups are run by Al Capone, who controls most of the city, and George 'Bugs' Moran, who is the third recent leader of the North Side Mob, the previous two having already been wiped out by Capone. With the aid of his main triggermen, Peter and Frank Gusenberg and James Clark, Moran carries out several attacks to muscle in on Capone's territory. Capone decides to wipe out Moran. Moran, however, carries out his plan to get the Mafia on his side, by wiping out Mafia head 'Patsy' Lolordo, and replacing him with their new ally, Joe Aiello. Once this happens, Capone tracks Aiello down and kills him before heading off to Miami. Meanwhile his head triggerman 'Machine Gun' Jack McGurn sets up Moran. On Valentine's Day, 1929, Moran is lured to his warehouse on the promise of a truckload of stolen hooch; Clark is mistaken for Moran and the massacre goes down, killing seven of Moran's men before Moran arrives. An epilogue explains that Moran died in jail of lung cancer, Capone of syphilis.

Background: Despite the $1 million price tag, Corman's biggest budget to date, *St Valentine's* was still Fox's lowest-budget film of the year. Determined to make it as authentic as possible, Corman hired Browne, who'd been a police reporter in Chicago at the time of the Capone's revenge-killing, to write the screenplay. Corman certainly made the most of his budget and sets from other major Fox productions. Capone's house was originally the manor in *The Sound Of Music;* the bar from *The Sand Pebbles* became a bar in a Chicago brothel; and the exterior sets from *Hello, Dolly!* were redressed to become downtown Twenties Chicago.

As usual, there were problems. The main one the casting. Corman had wanted Orson Welles to play Capone, with Robards as Moran. Fox protested, holding up Welles' reputation as a troublemaker. Robards could play Capone. At first, Corman tried to reason that Welles' build was perfect for Capone and likewise Robard's for Moran. But, realising he couldn't walk off another major project, he relented. Robards, although wary, agreed to play Capone (unfortunately, as he does chew the scenery rather). Corman had also wanted Jack Nicholson for one of the key roles but had to hire an actor under contact to Fox instead. He offered Nicholson a smaller role that meant a week and a half's work (the film – Corman's longest shoot yet – ran to thirty-five days) but Nicholson spotted a better role. It was a seven-week 'carry' as a getaway driver. It was a one-line part, but because the scenes he appeared in had to be shot in two locations over the length of the shoot, it meant that he would get paid for the entire seven weeks filming. Bruce Dern took a similar, financially-rewarding option.

Verdict: Despite Corman's hassles with Fox, the experience was a rewarding one. As always, he gets the entire budget on the screen and does an excellent job of capturing the look and feel of Twenties Chicago. Performances, with the exception of Robards', are uniformly superb, with Meeker, Segal and Ritchie outstanding. It remains a superior gangster movie. 5/5

The deal with Fox was a one-off and, for his next project, Corman returned to the relative freedom of AIP. Aware of the anti-Establishment credentials and commercial possibilities of making a movie about hippie drug culture which was then in full swing, Corman decided on a subject that the majors wouldn't have touched with a bargepole.

The Trip (1967)

Cast: Peter Fonda (Paul), Susan Strasberg (Sally), Bruce Dern (John), Dennis Hopper (Max), Salli Sasche (Glenn), Katherine Walsh (Lulu), Barboura Morris (Flo), Caren Bernsen (Alexandra), Dick Miller (Cash), Luana Anders (Waitress), Tommy Signorelli (Al), Mitzi Hoag (Wife), Judy Lang (Nadine), Barbara Renson (Helena), Susan Waters, Frankie Smith (Go-Go Girls).

Crew: Director/Producer Roger Corman, Writer Jack Nicholson, Cinematography Arch Dalzell, Music The American Flag, Editor Ronald Sinclair, Psychedelic Sequences Dennis Jakob, Psychedelic Effects Peter Gardiner, Alan Daviau, 85 minutes.

Story: Paul, a burned-out TV commercials director on the brink of divorce, drops acid for the first time under his friend John's guidance. During the trip, he experiences both good (meeting real-life drug guru Max, who forces him to examine his life, making love to Glenn, a woman he met at Max's house) and bad (being hunted in medieval times, a fear of death) – which John guides him through. When he thinks that John has died, he leaves the house and, believing himself hunted by hooded figures and cops, arrives on The Strip, a gaudy array of nightclubs, hippies, acid casualties and other nightlife. After fleeing a nightclub, he arrives at Max's. Max can't decide whether Paul's fear of cops is real or the trip, so he urges him to leave. Coming down, he flashes on all the incidents in his trip as he meets with Glenn. They go to her place and make love. The next day, he walks out onto the balcony to see the dawn. His life now at a crossroads, he feels reborn.

Background: For *The Trip*, Corman preferred not to rely on second-hand drug experiences. Instead, after reading Timothy Leary, he dropped acid himself. He gathered together some close friends, including Charles Griffith and his assistant Frances Doel, who was on hand to take notes. They drove up to Big Sur and Corman took the acid on a sugar cube while the others kept an eye on him. After a long time, during which he was convinced he had been ripped off, the LSD kicked in. By all accounts, he had an excellent seven-hour trip. Many of the images that came to him during it were integrated into Fonda's trip in the movie. Corman's trip was so good that he deliberately added some horror images (which harked back to his Poe cycle) to the movie in order not to appear too pro-LSD.

Griffith spent three months developing the screenplay, but neither of his final drafts satisfied Corman (the second was an opera, lyrics and all). Instead, he went to Jack Nicholson, who had also dropped acid, and was currently at a loose end in his acting career. Much of what Nicholson wrote had to be cut, mainly due to budgetary restrictions. Corman further upset him by giving Bruce Dern the role that Nicholson had written for himself. Hopper, who utters the most 'man's ever delivered in one speech (thirty-six, according to Corman's soundman), also did some filming for Corman. After the fifteen-day shoot was up, Corman sent him into the desert with Fonda and a hand-held camera. The footage was then cut into the medieval scenes, which were filmed at Big Sur. Many of the light effects came courtesy of Arch Dalzell, who tracked down a bunch of old trick lenses in a camera warehouse.

While Fonda and Hopper fully advocated the New Age that they believed was dawning, Corman took a dispassionate tone towards LSD's merits in the movie. Others were less certain that he'd achieved this. AIP were concerned that *The Trip* would be construed as a pro-LSD movie. Corman had already had problems with *The Wild Angels,* but this time the interference was more marked. Having turned in the answer print and gone to Europe to bale out *De Sade* (see below), Corman returned to find that not only had AIP (Corman accuses James Nicholson, who was the more conservative of the partnership) added a disclaimer representing their own antidrugs stance but they'd also edited some scenes and tampered with the film's ending. AIP re-cut Corman's careful dolly shots into a series of rapid cuts and then superimposed a jagged crack over the final shot of Fonda's face, implying that the trip had shattered his life.

Verdict: Despite AIP's editing, *The Trip* has worn reasonably well, particularly its comments on Vietnam and working-class America, but, as is always the case, second-hand drug experiences get a little tiring after a while. 3/5

If the movie upset AIP, the $6 million it took in rentals must have helped them recover. However, Corman, was rapidly becoming aware that, the more radical his films became, the more they were beginning to suffer at the hands of the distributors. *The Trip* was highly praised at Cannes but critics back home were less than supportive, with many conservative groups condemning it as being pro-drugs. In the UK, it was refused a certificate outright.

De Sade (1969)

Before his next proper film, Corman planned a movie on the life of the Marquis De Sade. It was scripted by Richard Matheson and given the green light by James Nicholson. But Corman immediately realised that there was a major problem with bringing the film to the screen. If they left in scenes depicting De Sade's fantasies, the film would be immediately refused distribution; if they left the scenes out, then the audience would be cheated. It was a no-win situation and Corman stepped down. Matheson did a second draft and the film was passed to Michael Reeves, who had done AIP proud with *Witchfinder General* (aka *The Conqueror Worm*, 1968). Reeves was undergoing shock therapy, and so the film was handed to Cy Endfield, director of *Zulu*. Filming went ahead, with a vaguely starry cast: Keir Dullea, Senta Berger, Lilli Palmer and John Huston. Endfield had his own problems, refusing to film the sex scenes. AIP producer, Louis Heyward, phoned Arkoff with the situation. Endfield ended up going into hospital suffering from exhaustion and Corman was brought back in to finish off the project. Wisely, he didn't take a credit. The film was an unwatchable mess that cheated its audience on a much higher level than just leaving out the sadism.

Target: Harry (1969)

aka *What's In It For Harry, How To Make It*

Cast: Vic Morrow (Harry Black), Suzanne Pleshette (Diane Reed), Victor Buono (Mosul Rashi), Cesar Romero (Lt George Duval), Stanley Holloway (Jason Carlyle), Charlotte Rampling (Ruth Carlyle), Michael Ansara (Major Milos Segora), Roger Corman (Man on Telephone).

Crew: Director Henry Neill (aka Roger Corman), Producer Gene Corman, Writer Bob Barbash, Cinematography Patrice Rouget, Music Les Baxter, Editor Monte Hellman, Production Design Sharon Compton, 81 minutes.

Story: Harry, a mercenary-cum-private eye, is hired to fly a forger from London to Istanbul, but others are only too keen to stop him...

Background: At the same time as *De Sade*, Corman also directed a TV movie. Intended as a series pilot, the series never took off because the pilot was considered too violent for broadcast. Corman came up with the idea after deciding he wanted to go to Istanbul and the best way to do this was to set a film there. *Target: Harry* finally gained a brief cinema release in the US and UK in 1979.

Verdict: Sorry, haven't been able to track it down.

Bloody Mama (1969)

Cast: Shelley Winters (Kate 'Ma' Barker), Pat Hingle (Sam Adams Pendlebury), Don Stroud (Herman Barker), Diane Varsi (Mona Gibson), Bruce Dern (Kevin Dirkman), Clint Kimbrough (Arthur Barker), Robert De Niro (Lloyd Barker), Robert Walden (Fred Barker), Alex Nicol (George Barker), Michael Fox (Dr Roth), Scatman Crothers (Moses), Stacy Harris (Agent McClellan), Pamela Dunlap (Rembrandt), Lisa Jill (Young Kate).

Crew: Director/Producer Roger Corman, Writers Robert Thom, Don Peters, Cinematography John A Alonzo, Music Don Randi, Editor Eve Newman, Special Effects A D Flowers, 90 minutes.

Story: Raped by her father as a young girl, Kate Barker vows to raise a family of boys who will suck by her no matter what. Her boys (psychotic Herman, bookish Arthur, junkie Lloyd and fey Freddie) certainly do, kept whipped, loyal and in incestuous thrall to their Ma. When hassled by the local sheriff after the rape of a local girl, Ma and her boys take off for better things, leaving behind George, the ineffectual father. They first survive by robbing people almost as dirt-poor as they are, but when Herman and Freddie are imprisoned for ripping off a charity hootenanny, their crimes escalate. Ma, Lloyd and Arthur hold up a bank to finance a lawyer to get them out of jail. This achieved, they move to easier times. Lloyd, increasingly hooked on heroin, blows this by kidnapping a girl he fancies. Drowning her, they move on and kidnap Sam Pendlebury, a rich cotton broker and a stroppy hostage, to boot. Fearing Pendlebury can identify them, Ma's plan is to execute him but the boys free him when they get the ransom. At their next hideout, they are reported for killing a local sharecropper's pig (I kid you not), the Feds close in and the entire family are killed in the ensuing shoot-out.

Background: At this stage, Corman was beginning to feel burned out. He'd passed on plenty of scripts that failed to catch his interest, but *Bloody Mama* had potential. He hired Don Peters to polish Robert Thom's script and negotiated a four-week shoot. Filmed on location in the Ozarks and Little Rock, Arkansas, Corman chose a photographer who would be able to give the movie a realistic feel. He hired John A Alonzo who, until then, had mainly been filming Jacques Cousteau documentaries.

Both Corman and James Nicholson agreed that Shelley Winters should play Ma Barker. When she accepted, both she and Corman worked on the casting. More a character study than a coherent narrative, *Bloody Mama* benefited from the actors that were hired. Winters got De Niro cast on the strength of his performance in *Greetings* by Brian De Palma. Both Winters and De Niro were dedicated Method actors. Their performances in the movie reflect the extent to which they immersed themselves in their roles but it took its toll on them. Winters, who would play arias on set to get into character, sat up all night in a funeral parlour in a nearby town to prepare for the funeral of De Niro's character. To replicate the effects of his character's junkie lifestyle, De Niro went on a diet that consisted of little more than water and fruit juice. For one scene, where De Niro was driving a period getaway car, both Alonzo and Corman were strapped to its fenders with fireman belts. The car went screaming downhill with De Niro driving like mad. At some point near the last take of the scene, Winters said to him: 'You're doing great, you're really looking like a guy driving out of control.' 'I *am* driving out of control,' De Niro replied, 'I have no idea how to drive.' He hadn't mentioned it because he didn't want Corman to get a stunt driver.

AIP again interfered with Corman's final version cutting three minutes of material from the movie before release. However, the final straw had yet to come.

Verdict: The plot of *Bloody Mama* is really incidental to the representation of this horrific family's dynamics at work. Corman applies plenty of zooms and fast edits to heighten the action, but perhaps the most telling detail of the picture is the group of townsfolk who arrive to have a picnic and witness the climactic shoot-out. Yeah, we're all voyeurs. 4/5

Gas-s-s-s, Or It Became Necessary To Destroy The World In Order To Save It (1970)

aka *Gas! Or It Became Necessary To Destroy The World In Order To Save It*

Cast: Robert Corff (Coel), Elaine Giftos (Cilla), Pat Patterson (Demeter), George Armitage (Billy The Kid), Alex Wilson (Jason), Alan Braunstein (Dr Drake), Ben Vereen (Carlos), Cindy Williams (Marissa), Bud Cort (Hooper), Talia Coppola (aka Talia Shire) (Coralie), Country Joe McDonald (FM Radio), Lou Procopio (Marshall McLuhan), Jackie Farley (Ginnie), Phil Borneo (Quant), David Osterhout (Texas Ranger), Bruce Karcher (Edgar Allan Poe).

Crew: Producer/Director Roger Corman, Writer George Armitage, Cinematography Ron Dexter, Music Country Joe And The Fish, Barry Melton, Editor George Van Noy, Art Director Dave Nichols, 79 minutes.

Story: After the accidental release of a secret army gas, everyone over 25 dies. The children begin to form their own cliques and groups but many simply follow the social patterns established by their parents. Coel and Cilla leave Dallas before the police can clamp down. With others that they meet along the way they try to reach a commune established in New Mexico. On the road they encounter the godlike rock star FM Radio, worshipped as (and interrupted by) God, Edgar Allan Poe and middle-class Hell's Angels who protect their country club territory on golf carts. They are captured both by a fascist football team and Marshall McLuhan before finally reaching the commune.

Background: Gas-s-s-s was Corman's last film for AIP, not only because he needed a break from directing, but for other reasons. He planned *Gas-s-s-s* as 'an apocalyptic, Strangelovian political satire' and, oddly enough, it was based on an idea floated by James Nicholson. He, in turn, had been inspired by the hippy slogan: 'Never trust anyone over thirty' (the same phrase that would inspire AIP's *Wild In The Streets*). Although Corman was working with George Armitage on the script, he was already committed to direct *Von Richtofen And Brown* in the spring of the following year. As a result, he had to go into production on *Gas-s-s-s* without a finished script. Corman brought Armitage along by casting him as Billy The Kid, so he could keep on rewriting.

The filming moved from Dallas (where they recreated JFK's assassination) to New Mexico and then was supposed to finish atop the Acoma Indian Pueblo, a mesa in New Mexico. But from the outset, everything seemed to be against them. They suffered heavy sleet in Dallas. They managed to reach the virtually inaccessible mesa, only for the Native Americans to demand more money for filming on their ancestral homeland. The Grateful Dead were booked to play the drive-in gig, but suddenly doubled their fee, so Corman hired Country Joe And The Fish instead. Go, Jerry. On the LBJ Freeway in Dallas, which was yet to be opened to the public, filming had to be stopped briefly when a cop interrupted. The apocalyptic nature of the movie meant that production assistant Paul Rapp had had fifty smashed cars towed there at $10 a pop. The cop said they'd received five hundred calls about a major road accident.

These combined setbacks depressed Corman throughout the shoot. On the last day, filming the climactic scene at the mesa, the first take was an utter mess. Corman said nothing. Rapp got everyone back into their positions for a second take and this time everything went perfectly. In Corman's autobiography, Rapp recalls: 'Roger got up from his chair slowly, thanked everybody, and said very quietly, "Let's go home."'

It wasn't over, though. The climactic scene had encompassed almost everything in his career. Hell, his *life*. He had the Native Americans, an entire marching band from a local high school, Hell's Angels in golf carts, a football team, Poe, God. He even allowed the leading man to kiss the woman, something he'd never used before because it was a cliché, this time included precisely because it was a cliché. This was a massive celebration, with a panoramic shot stretching nearly sixty miles across New Mexico. And AIP cut it. They stopped the film at the couple's kiss because God's commentary on the film's climax upset them. Again, Corman blamed the increasingly conservative Nicholson. Again, Corman was out of the country, filming *Von Richtofen And Brown*, when the cuts were made. He only found out when he attended *Gas-s-s-s* screening at the Edinburgh Festival.

Verdict: The above 'story' can't really cover what is, in effect, a series of mickey-takings on various aspects of the American Way of Life. This scattershot approach doesn't always work, and it hasn't aged as well as, say, Robert Altman's *Nashville* or Hal Ashby's *Harold And Maude*. Yet Corman had proved his ability to mix humour with 'difficult' subject matter a long time before and here pulls it off, in grand style, one last time. 3/5

Von Richtofen And Brown (1970)

aka *The Red Baron*

Cast: John Phillip Law (Baron Manfred Von Richtofen), Don Stroud (Roy Brown), Barry Primus (Hermann Goering), Karen Huston (Ilse), Corin Redgrave (Lance Hawker), Hurd Hatfield (Fokker), Peter Masterson (Oswald Boelcke), Robert La Tourneaux (Udet), George Armitage (Wolff), Steve McHattie (Voss), Brian Foley (Lothar Von Richtofen), David Osterhout (Holzapfel), Clint Kimbrough (Von Hoeppner), Gordon Phillips (Cargonico), Ferdy Mayne (Richtofen's Father), Maureen Cusack (Richtofen's Mother).

Crew: Director Roger Corman, Producer Gene Corman, Writers John and Joyce Corrington, Cinematography Michael Reed, Music Hugo Friedhofer, Editors George Van Noy, Alan Collins. Special Effects Peter Dawson, 97 minutes.

Story: Nervous Canadian pilot Roy Brown vows to bring down chivalrous fighter ace Baron Manfred von Richtofen. While Von Richtofen adheres to a code that his contemporaries think ridiculous, including using a plane of lower power painted red rather than camouflaged, Brown is rendered nauseous by the thought of flying and has to down a quart of milk to calm his ulcers. Brown infuriates Von Richtofen with a sneak attack that destroys many German planes and kills innocent people. He instigates a counter-attack that kills a group of Canadian nurses. With Germany on the brink of losing the war, Von Richtofen is asked to help overthrow the government. He refuses and goes on one last mission, looking for a final showdown with Brown. Brown wins.

Background: Shot in Ireland for under $1 million over six weeks, *Von Richtofen* was the last film Corman would direct officially for nearly twenty years. Two other World War I flying movies had been recently filmed in Ireland, John Guillermin's *The Blue Max* (1966) and Blake Edwards' *Darling Lili* (1970), and Corman struck a deal to hire the planes they had used.

Each film's flying sequences had taken several months to film, Corman aimed to do his in two weeks. For these, he used three separate units shooting the aerial sequences simultaneously. For the first, he had a thirty-foot-high platform built to shoot low-flying planes, so it looked as if the camera was also airborne. The second unit was filmed by art director Jimmy Murakami from an Air Force helicopter. The third unit was covered from an aerial-survey plane hired from an oil company, capable of flying at any altitude at very low speeds, it gave Corman a chance to control filming the dog-fights close up. Two of the planes were two-seaters, which allowed Corman to sit the actors behind the pilots and bolt an Arriflex camera between the two. When the time came, the actors would turn on the camera. This provided much more convincing (and cheaper) flight sequences than filming these scenes as matte shots. In true Corman style, even Corman's production assistant (soon Mrs Corman), Julie Halloran, got in on the act. Filming the raid on the German airbase, he found they were a gunner short. Halloran grabbed a helmet and climbed on board.

Verdict: As you might gather from the above, the flying sequences are great to look at, excellently choreographed and skilfully edited. Unfortunately, when the film isn't airborne, it comes down to earth with a bump. 3/5

6: In Production

'People are fond of leaving Roger and doing other things and talking about how Roger loused up their movie by interfering too much, but then, if you really look back at it, if Roger made your rubber-fish movie a little worse, or your women-in-cages movie a little worse, whatever he did, in the long run it probably was more beneficial than you originally thought at the time, and was certainly worth the experience.'

Joe Dante

Following *Von Richtofen and Brown* Corman knew that he was burned out from directing, which was hardly surprising, in the past sixteen years he had directed 49 movies and produced and overseen countless other pictures. While his work rate had slowed over the years, it was still time for a change of direction. Corman's last few experiences with an increasingly interventionist AIP had proved this to him. The more ambitious the picture, the greater the interference that it had invited. With this in mind, he started another production company. This time, he wouldn't direct the pictures that it released, rather he would produce, or even executive produce, its output. But, unlike Filmgroup, the company's name would become synonymous with his. So much so that the company, even after its dissolution, would forever be remembered as the Corman Academy of Film-Making. It would form the blueprint for companies such as New Line, Charles Band's Empire (and Full Moon), the Weinstein Brothers' Miramax and even, god help us, Lloyd Kaufman's Troma: small production companies homing in on exploitation opportunities and using each success as a building block to finance more movies and pick up films for distribution that they believed in. Just as AIP had done before them. Corman called his company New World; its 'alumni' are still with us today.

With no fresh exploitable trends around, Corman and his staff set out to forge some new ones. They made soft-porn/socially aware movies about student nurses (*The Student Nurses*, *Private Duty Nurses*, *Candy Stripe Nurses*, etc.), they made women-in-prison movies (*The Big Doll House*, *Caged Heat*, etc), they made car–chase movies, Hell's Angels movies, gangster movies... In short, they made anything that could be produced cheaply and turn a tidy profit.

New World's other claim to fame was that they were instrumental in distributing many important foreign-language titles in the US. Previously, 'art' movies had generally been distributed by small companies with little distribution muscle, or divisions at major studios where the films tended to be poorly handled. New World already had a strong reputation in distribution and could therefore book such movies into larger circuits. Their first was Ingmar Bergman's *Cries And Whispers*, which did well enough for Corman to continue picking up movies, either on the recommendations of his trusted sales managers, Frank Moreno and Barbara Boyle, or, in some cases, on the name of the director. Other successful releases included Fellini's *Amarcord*, Volker Schlöndorff's *The Tin Drum* and Truffaut's *The Story Of Adele H.* These films not only raised New World beyond being a purely exploitation company, they also brought in a lot of revenue. Plus, many of them won Best Foreign Film Oscars – another feather in the company's cap.

Time, and Corman's enthusiasm, was running out for New World. When the company had started, major studios would platform their releases. This meant that their A films would be screened at one or two cinemas in each city for their opening weeks and then gradually filtered down to more provincial cinemas, their audiences drawn by cheaper tickets and second features of the type supplied by New World. Two changes had occurred since then. Firstly the majors had started releasing their films into hundreds of cinemas in their first week – many of them in the new shopping malls in the provinces. The increased audiences from this tactic negated the need for second features. Secondly, the success of films such as *Star Wars* and *Jaws* showed the majors that there was no longer any shame in making their own exploitation movies.

In 1982, Corman sold New World to a consortium of lawyers. For the past couple of years it had begun to show a loss for the first time. The majors had cottoned onto its success and begun making similar movies, but on budgets in millions, rather than hundred thousands. Corman sold it for around $16.5 million but held onto the back catalogue and his production crew. The buyers got the name and the distribution.

Corman's aim was to go straight back into production, with New World distributing his movies. The result was law suits all round. Corman sued New World in 1985 for not paying him the money his productions were making. New World counter-sued Corman for going back into distribution, something he hadn't wanted to do anyway, but circumstances had forced him into. New World settled out of court. Corman got his money and was allowed to go back into distribution.

His first idea was to set up a joint distribution company with four independent producers, something that would remove much of the onerous distribution business from his shoulders. But one by one they all backed out.

Corman went back into business on his own – this time with Concorde-New Horizons.

Unlike the New World era, many of these films were designed to be straight-to-video titles, possibly with a minimal cinema release. Many were sword-and-sorcery, sf/horror or martial arts pictures, usually incorporating maximum violence and just enough nudity to allow them an R-rating. There was an unsuccessful remake of *The Masque Of The Red Death* in 1988 and sequels to some of the cultier New World titles, such as *Slumber Party Massacre 2* and *Hollywood Boulevard 2*. It also diversified into family-oriented movies *(Andy Colby's Incredible Adventure, Munchies, etc.)*.

In 1990, Corman made a brief return to directing.

Roger Corman's Frankenstein Unbound (1990)

Cast: John Hurt (Dr Buchanan), Raul Julia (Dr Frankenstein), Bridget Fonda (Mary Godwin), Nick Brimble (Frankenstein's Monster), Catherine Rabett (Elizabeth), Jason Patric (Lord Byron), Michael Hutchence (Percy Shelley), Catherine Corman (Justine), Mickey Knox (General), Terri Treas (Voice Of Car).

Crew: Director/Co-producer/Co-Writer Roger Corman, Co-Producers Thom Mount, Kabi Jaeger, Co-Writers F X Feeny, (Uncredited) Ed Neumeir, Novel Brian Aldiss, Cinematography Armando Nannuzzi, Michael Scott, Music Carl Davis, Editors Jay Cassidy, Mary Bauer, Production Design Enrico Tovaglieri, Special Effects Nick Dudman, 85 minutes.

Story: New LA, 2031. Scientist Buchanan tests his latest atomic weapon, which accidentally causes a rent in the time-space continuum. Buchanan and his computerised car are sucked into a time-slip and emerge near Lake Geneva in 1813. In a local inn, he encounters Baron Frankenstein. Following him, he witnesses Frankenstein conversing with his monster. The creature has already killed Frankenstein's brother, William, and threatens to kill his fiancée, Elizabeth, unless Frankenstein makes him a mate. Frankenstein's maid is found guilty of killing William and Buchanan tries to get Frankenstein to admit his own guilt to save her. When this fails, Buchanan visits the Villa Deodati, where he meets Lord Byron, Percy Shelley and Mary Godwin. His knowledge of Mary's novel impresses her as she hasn't completed it yet. Their romance is brief, but neither can save the maid, or stop Frankenstein. Pursuing Frankenstein and the monster himself, Buchanan witnesses Elizabeth's murder and resurrection as the creature's mate, just as another time-slip hits. In snowy wastes, at the last outpost of humanity, Frankenstein kills Elizabeth, the monster kills Frankenstein and, after a frantic pursuit, Buchanan destroys the monster. He heads off into the snow, alone.

Background: Universal had already approached Corman once, with market research that a film titled *Roger Corman's Frankenstein* would be successful with movie-goers. He rejected the offer because he believed there were more than enough movie versions of Frankenstein already. He passed a second time a year later. A year later he was approached by Robert Thom, Universal's former head of production, who had gone independent (he also wrote *Bloody Mama*). This time, Corman agreed to direct, but only if they could adapt Brian Aldiss' novel, which had added a fresh slant to the Frankenstein myth. Buchanan was changed from a retired diplomat to a scientist in order to draw a clear parallel between him and Frankenstein. Originally, the movie was shorter than his contract demanded; Corman added some extra scenes, and tweaked the movie further after a sneak preview. Well-received in America, it didn't fare so well critically in Europe and the UK.

Verdict: Corman keeps to the spirit of Aldiss' book and Julia and Hurt play the adversaries with enthusiasm. However the ham-fisted dialogue (Brimble's monster frequently sounds like Tubbs from *The League of Gentlemen*), the *Knightrider* car and the regrettable Poe-cycle-style dream sequences pretty much kill the movie. The latter suggest that Corman was picking up almost where he left off, with nothing new to offer. A pity. 1/5

Apart from an abortive commercial for Greenpeace in 1996 (which ran into trouble for its images of naked children – not Corman's idea – dragging media concerns over paedophilia into view), Corman hasn't directed since.

When the video market began to bottom out, Corman struck a deal with Showtime, the cable TV network, to produce a series of TV movies under the banner 'Roger Corman Presents'. Several of the films would be remakes of his old movies, including *The Wasp Woman*, *Not Of This Earth* (already remade in 1988 by Jim Wynorski) and *A Bucket Of Blood*. Others would be remakes of New World movies, including *Humanoids From The Deep* and *Piranha*. While *Bucket* and *Wasp* manage to retain a certain amount of sly humour, the rest of the package is fairly poor. *Piranha* is a particularly pointless exercise. Most of the dialogue is taken straight from John Sayles' original (but uncredited) script but played miserably straight, while the effects come straight from the original movie. Other TV mini-series have followed, such as *The Phantom Eye* in 1999 and *The Black Scorpion* in 2001.

To go into further depth about Corman's output as a producer would probably take another two books, and, despite some entertaining movies, it would not be an enlivening experience. As time at Concorde-New Horizons has progressed, turnover is as rapid as it was when Corman was directing for AIP, but the age of the classic exploitation movie is now long over.

There are only so many sequels to *Bloodfist* or *Deathstalker* that any one person can watch before wanting to give up living. While Corman continues to nurture new talent, albeit less successfully (recent examples include Katt Shea – *Poison Ivy* and Rodman Flender – *Idle Hands*), his influence now seems to be mainly as a moneyman and many of the ideas that are green-lighted seem woefully weak. The sad fact is that he's still competing with major studios that can out-budget him, but nowadays, they frequently out-Corman him as well.

7: The Roger Corman Academy Of Film Technique

One of the many unofficial names given to those poor souls who laboured under Corman's tutelage, Corman's own movies and his later production companies proved a fine breeding ground for future Hollywood talent. If you could make it there, you'd make it anywhere...

Peter Bogdanovich

Having shot scenes to Americanise Corman's Russian sf purchase *Planeta Burg* (as *Voyage To The Planet Of The Prehistoric Women*), Corman offered Bogdanovich his own movie. The conditions were that Bogdanovich used twenty minutes from *The Terror*, another twenty minutes of new footage with Karloff and forty minutes with other actors, giving Corman a new Karloff movie. The opportunity had arisen when Karloff's agent had discovered that *The Terror* had made more money than originally realised and tried to renegotiate Karloff's take. Corman had agreed, on condition that the actor gave him another two days' work on a future film. In the end, Bogdanovich got Karloff for four days and used the footage for *The Terror* at his film's climax, as the film showing at the drive-in. Released in 1968, the film was *Targets*, a chilling combination of American gun-culture and Old World horror. Bogdanovich went on to direct *The Last Picture Show* and *Mask* among others.

Francis Ford Coppola

Coppola had previously impressed Corman by creating aliens that looked like genitalia as inserts (sic) for his Russian sf import *Nebo Zoyvot*, which became *Battle Beyond The Sun*. Coppola was hired as soundman for *The Young Racers* and willingly went for the job because he knew that, whenever Corman took a crew overseas, it meant that he would personally finance a second picture on the back of the first. After a pitching battle between Coppola and Menachem Golan, Corman went for Coppola's idea, mainly because it would be cheaper. The result was the taut horror movie *Dementia 13*. Coppola returned the favour by casting Corman as a senator in *The Godfather Part 2*.

Martin Scorsese

Scorsese had recently completed *Who's That Knocking On My Door?* and was working with John Cassevetes on the sound effects for *Minnie And Moskowitz* when Corman hired him to make *Boxcar Bertha*, ostensibly a sequel to *Bloody Mama*. Given a budget of under $1 million, Scorsese shot the movie in Arkansas. The executives at AIP were unnerved when the first four days' rushes proved to be entirely of train wheels going round. They tried to pressure Corman into sacking Scorsese and directing *Boxcar* himself. Corman stood firm and his faith was rewarded.

Joe Dante/Allan Arkush

Dante and Arkush worked as trailers editors for New World, frequently cutting in stock footage from other movies to make the trailers look more exciting. They landed their first directing job as the result of a bet between Corman and producer Jon Davison that Davison couldn't make a movie for $90,000, a budget lower than any New World movie. Realising they could only afford to have people talking for that amount, the pair set the movie in an exploitation movie company and intercut as much stock action footage from other New World movies as they could get away with. *Hollywood Boulevard* barely broke even, but it got the pair further directing work at New World. Dante made the *Jaws* cash-in *Piranha*, and Arkush the Fifties teen rebellion pastiche *Rock 'N' Roll High School*. As a sort of tribute, Dante gave Corman a cameo in *The Howling*. After Dee Wallace has vacated a phone booth, Corman checks the reject slot for change.

John Sayles

The future screenwriter and director of *The Brother From Another Planet* and *Lone Star* was hired by Corman's assistant, Francis Doel, on the strength of some published short stories. Sayles was paid $10,000 to rewrite the script for *Piranha*. He later wrote New World's *Star Wars* cash-in, *Battle Beyond The Stars*, which was basically *The Seven Samurai* in space.

Jonathan Kaplan

Graduating from NYU in 1970, Kaplan was hired on Scorsese's recommendation. His first film for New World was *Night Call Nurses*. At the screening of the first cut, Kaplan was convinced that his career was over. However, Corman went through the film with him, suggesting various edits to help improve it. Kaplan went on to direct two other New World pictures and later made *The Accused* and *Brokedown Palace*. He's also a regular director on *ER*.

Jonathan Demme

The future director of *The Silence Of The Lambs* and *Philadelphia* had previously worked as Corman's publicist for *Von Richtofen And Brown*. For New World he wrote *Angels Hard As They Come* (which he pitched as *Rashomon* on motorcycles) and *The Hot Box*. He spent a year scripting *Caged Heat* by which time the market for women-in-prison movies was waning. Demme managed to get his own finance and Corman agreed to distribute it. Demme gave Corman several cameo appearances in his movies, notably FBI Director Hayden Burke in *Lambs*.

James Cameron

Future 'king of the world' *Titanic* director Cameron worked on *Battle Beyond The Stars*. Horrified by the special-effects budgets he was being quoted, Corman set up his own in-house special-effects company. Hired by the head of the company, Cameron worked as model builder, effects cameraman, pyrotechnician and art director.

Gale Anne Hurd

Hired on the basis of her film criticism, Hurd worked as production assistant on *Humanoids From The Deep* and moved up to assistant production manager on *Battle Beyond The Stars*, where she met James Cameron. Later Mrs (and ex-Mrs) Cameron, they worked together on *The Terminator* and *T2*. Hurd's most recent production is Ang Lee's forthcoming version of *The Incredible Hulk*.

Ron Howard

Howard was still starring in *Happy Days* when he acted in New World's *Eat My Dust*. Wanting to move into directing, Howard pitched several ideas to Corman but he didn't bite. Instead he asked Howard to come up with a movie around the title *Grand Theft Auto*. Corman gave Howard thorough advice on directing the film, ending with the prophetic message 'If you do a really good job on this picture, you will never work for me again.' Howard gave Corman a walk-on part as a congressman in the bloated *Apollo 13*.

Amy Jones

She started out editing trailers alongside Dante and Arkush (and helped them salvage *Hollywood Boulevard*). Looking to move into directing, Jones read Rita Mae Brown's script for feminist slasher *Slumber Party Massacre*. She got together a group of film students and some unused remnants of film from short reels and shot the first seven pages. She edited it on Joe Dante's moviola while he was working on *The Howling*. Dante recommended her film to Corman, who liked what he saw and gave her the budget to film the rest. As Amy Holden-Jones, she later scripted *Beethoven* and *Indecent Proposal*.

Paul Bartel

Hired to direct *Death Race 2000*, a *Rollerball* cash-in scripted by Robert Thom and Charles Griffith, Bartel's original version was more comedic than Corman wanted. So he cut much of Bartel's material and got Griffith to shoot violent inserts. The film featured early roles for David Carradine and Sylvester Stallone. Although Bartel continued to work at New World it was only as a character actor for his friends' pictures such as *Piranha* and *Rock 'n' Roll High School*. Bartel's finest film remains *Eating Raoul*. He died of liver cancer in 2001.

Lewis Teague

The director of John Sayles *The Lady In Red* and *Alligator,* Teague worked as editor on Monte Hellman's *Cockfighter* and got his first directing break filming genuine cockfighting inserts for the movie.

Monte Hellman

One of America's great lost directors, Hellman worked second unit on several Corman films, making his directorial debut in 1959 on the Corman-produced *Beast From Haunted Cave*. He went on to direct two great absurdist westerns (*Ride In The Whirlwind* and *The Shooting*) both produced by Corman and starring Jack Nicholson, as well as the excellent road movie *Two-Lane Blacktop*. Never well received by American audiences, his last directing job was *Silent Night, Bloody Night 3*.

8: Cormedia

Bibliography

Several books about Corman are now out of print, including Ed Naha's *The Films Of Roger Corman: Brilliance On A Budget*, Charles Flynn and Todd McCarthy's *Roger Corman: King Of The B's* and Stéphane Bourgoin's *Roger Corman*. There are still several good titles available.

How I Made A Hundred Movies In Hollywood And Never Lost A Dime by Roger Corman with Jim Jerome, US: Da Capo Press, 1998, Paperback, 242 pages, $14.95, ISBN 0306808749. Not as self-aggrandising as you expect, Corman's autobiography cheerfully whips through his career with several ego-popping quotes from associates such as Beach Dickerson, Dick Miller, Joe Dante, Coppola and Scorsese.

Roger Corman: The Best Of The Cheap Acts by Mark Thomas McGee, US: McFarland & Company, Inc., 1988, Paperback, 250 pages, $25.95, ISBN 0786404779. Excellent overview of Corman's work which cuts off at the sale of New World. Includes detailed filmography and potted biographies of Corman's rep company.

The Films Of Roger Corman: 'Shooting My Way Out Of Trouble' by Alan Frank, UK: B T Batsford Ltd, 1998, Paperback, 194 pages, £17.99, ISBN 0713482729. The respected film critic weighs in with this eminently browsable title covering Corman's directorial output, fleshed out with lots of rare stills.

Roger Corman – An Unauthorized Biography Of The Godfather Of Indie Filmmaking by Beverly Gray, US: Renaissance Books, 2000, Hardback, 306 pages, $23.95, ISBN 1580631460. Corman as insecure, manipulative letch – as written by ex-development executive Gray, after she was fired so Corman could hire someone cheaper. However, it's not all assassination. The book fully covers his Concorde-New Horizons period and contains many new interviews with Corman staff.

Easy Riders, Raging Bulls by Peter Biskind, UK: Bloomsbury, 1999, Paperback, 512 pages, £8.99, ISBN 0747544212. Biskind's mighty deconstruction of Sixties and Seventies cinema necessarily includes entries on Corman, by way of showing up Coppola, Scorsese and Spielberg as very disturbed people. A must-read.

Flying Through Hollywood By The Seat Of My Pants by Samuel Z Arkoff and Richard Trubo, US: Birch Lane Press, 1992, Hardback, 206 pages, $15.95, ISBN 1559721073. The vice-president of AIP holds forth in this brisk but all-too restrained reminiscence. Tales of economic hardship abound but you can't help feeling he's holding back…

Scorsese On Scorsese edited by David Thomson and Ian Christie, UK: faber and faber, 1989, Paperback, 180 pages, £6.99, ISBN 0571152430. Chapter 2 covers Scorsese's relationship with Corman while making *Boxcar Bertha.*

It Conquered The Web

Type 'Roger Corman' into any search engine and watch those sites pop up. Many, however, just contain potted biographies that are, obviously, superfluous after reading this book (ahem). However, among the sites worth checking out are:

New Concorde – http://www.newconcorde.com.html -- Corman's very own corporate site offers a filmography, scenarios and online video ordering facilities, as well as a rather cringe-inducing biog of the man himself.

Bright Lights -- http://www.brightlightsfilm.com/27/cormaninterview1.html -- This lively film site has a 1974 interview with Corman talking candidly about New World.

The Onion -- http://www.theavclub.com/avclub3512/avfeature3512.html -- The king of the satirical newspapers has a similarly ironic website. They interviewed Corman in depth in 1999, a transcript of which can be found at this address.

Images Journal -- http://www.imagesjournal.com/issue09/features/rogercorman/ -- Chunky type makes this movie website rather hard to read, but Andrew Rausch's interview with Corman about his alumni is worth checking out.

Internet Movie Database -- http://www.imdb.com/Name?Corman,+Roger -- Think Corman's directorial output was exhausting? Then check out his production credits in full. This exhaustive listing details movies, personnel, box-office takings, locations, cameos and more. But it's not just for Corman; everyone in the movie industry gets the same treatment.

The Other Cinema -- http://www.othercinema.com/otherzine/otherzine4/corman.html -- Dedicated to exploitation and extreme cinema, this site carries a translation of an essay that Corman wrote for a French anthology on Surrealism.

The Astounding B Monster -- http://www.bmonster.com -- Beautifully designed sight dedicated to explotation cinema. No Corman interview but there are lengthy and revealing chats with Jackie Joseph, Susan Cabot, Mel Welles and Pamela Duncan, amongst others.

The Essential Library: Currently Available

Film Directors:

Woody Allen (2nd)	**Tim Burton**	**Ang Lee**
Jane Campion*	**John Carpenter**	**Joel & Ethan Coen (2nd)**
Jackie Chan	**Steven Soderbergh**	**Clint Eastwood**
David Cronenberg	**Terry Gilliam***	**Michael Mann**
Alfred Hitchcock (2nd)	**Krzysztof Kieslowski***	**Roman Polanski**
Stanley Kubrick (2nd)	**Sergio Leone**	**Oliver Stone**
David Lynch	**Brian De Palma***	**George Lucas**
Sam Peckinpah*	**Ridley Scott (2nd)**	**James Cameron**
Orson Welles (2nd)	**Billy Wilder**	**Roger Corman**
Steven Spielberg	**Mike Hodges**	**Spike Lee**

Film Genres:

Blaxploitation Films	**Bollywood**	**French New Wave**
Horror Films	**Spaghetti Westerns**	**Vietnam War Movies**
Slasher Movies	**Film Noir**	**Hammer Films**
Vampire Films*	**Heroic Bloodshed***	**Carry On Films**
German Expressionist Films		

Film Subjects:

Laurel & Hardy	**Marx Brothers**	**Film Music**
Steve McQueen*	**Marilyn Monroe**	**The Oscars® (2nd)**
Filming On A Microbudget	**Bruce Lee**	**Writing A Screenplay**
Film Studies		

Music:

The Madchester Scene	**Beastie Boys**	**Jethro Tull**
How To Succeed In The Music Business		

Literature:

Cyberpunk	**Philip K Dick**	**The Beat Generation**
Agatha Christie	**Sherlock Holmes**	**Noir Fiction***
Terry Pratchett	**Hitchhiker's Guide (2nd)**	**Alan Moore**
William Shakespeare	**Creative Writing**	**Tintin**

Ideas:

Conspiracy Theories	**Nietzsche**	**UFOs**
Feminism	**Freud & Psychoanalysis**	**Bisexuality**

History:

Alchemy & Alchemists	**The Crusades**	**The Black Death**
Jack The Ripper	**The Rise Of New Labour**	**Ancient Greece**
American Civil War	**American Indian Wars**	**Witchcraft**
Globalisation	**Who Shot JFK?**	

Miscellaneous:

Stock Market Essentials	**How To Succeed As A Sports Agent**	**Doctor Who**

Available at bookstores or send a cheque (payable to 'Oldcastle Books') to: **Pocket Essentials (Dept RC), P O Box 394, Harpenden, Herts, AL5 1XJ, UK**. £3.99 each (£2.99 if marked with an *). For each book add 50p(UK)/£1 (elsewhere) postage & packing